MW00875872

Singing Beyond Sorrow

A Year of Grief, Gratitude & Grace

Carole Marie Downing

Grateful Heart Books

Portland, Oregon

Carole Marie Downing / Grateful Heart Books

www.gratefulheartcoaching.com

Publisher's Note: The intention of this book is to share information in a general way and is a personal perspective on the nature of grief. The author of this book is not a licensed medical or mental health professional and does not intend for the information in this book to be used in place of professional medical, physical, emotional or mental health treatment.

Designations used to distinguish a company or products are claimed as trademarks of the respective company or trademark owner. Where those designations appear in this book, they have been identified with initial capital letters.

Ordering Information: Quantity sales. Special discounts are available on quantity purchases by corporations, associations, and others. For details, contact the author through the website above.

Grateful Heart Books / Carole Marie Downing. -- 1st ed.
ISBN 978-1512209518

*For Michael
and his legacy of loving*

*and for those who walked with us
on this journey ~ thank you.*

CONTENTS

The Unbroken
- By Rashani Réa

There is a brokenness
out of which comes the unbroken,
a shatteredness out of which blooms the unshatterable.

There is a sorrow
beyond all grief which leads to joy
and a fragility out of whose depths emerges strength.

There is a hollow space too vast for words
through which we pass with each loss,
out of whose darkness we are sanctioned into being.

There is a cry deeper than all sound
whose serrated edges cut the heart
as we break open
to the place inside which is unbreakable
and whole,
while learning to sing.

Introduction

The two of us were sitting outside on the deck, the warmth of a spring afternoon weaving around us by way of a gentle wind. For a long time we were quiet—any words either too heavy or not important enough to say. And then my husband, Michael, broke the silence, saying, with a smile, "I should have thought more about the consequences when I married a hospice nurse."

As always with him, it was just enough humor to briefly overcome my concerns and make me laugh. We both laughed, and then, finally, we cried. We then started the conversation of how to live the last days of his life.

It turned out there weren't as many days as we had hoped. A short month later, I was sitting alone on our deck, speaking out into the darkness of the summer evening and trying desperately to feel his presence on the other side of the veil that now separated us.

I had never imagined how some day all that training in nursing would be needed for the one moment that mattered most in my life. The moment of his death defined me. I knew it had altered my life in a way that I had yet to understand. I wondered which moment mattered more, or was more profound: the moment I met him or the moment he died? I didn't know, but I can say both moments changed my life forever.

I met Michael on a cold Alaskan evening at an art gallery. I walked into the warmth of the gallery after the bracing the cool air, and the first thing I saw were his bright eyes shining out at me from across the room. In that moment, love at first sight became real for me. He was talking with a friend of mine. The electricity of instant connection pulled me over to create an introduction. As soon as we met, the rest of the room faded away. He was magnetic, handsome, charming, and kind. So kind. By the end of the evening, I knew I was in love. We were engaged within two months, married within eight, and pregnant by the end of the year. At age thirty-six, I had given up on the possibility of marriage and children, but when I met him it all not only seemed possible, but absolutely right.

I wondered sometimes why my life with him was forever on fast-forward. We married so quickly and had our son, Lucas, shortly after. We moved twice in two years and bought a home in Portland with the future plan of moving again to build a home on Bainbridge Island, just west of Seattle. He was a man of action, fitting years of living into what felt like weeks. It made me dizzy to keep up, but the energy of his loving infused our lives and everything he touched was successful. How could I argue? And now, in retrospect, I see that perhaps some deep part of him knew he didn't have much time.

When the diagnosis of cancer came, the timeline was short. In the beginning, we were hopeful and determined to beat the odds. Lucas was only five, and it was impossible to believe that Michael wouldn't be there to see him grow up. We sought second opinions and tried everything in all spectrums of medicine and the healing arts for a cure. He went running every day and worked full-time through a year of treatment and chemotherapy. He lived fully despite the cancer, and his intention to find a cure was strong.

I knew we would need a miracle. And in the end, the physical cure we hoped for didn't happen. There was healing, though. Deep healing. Eventually we both accepted that he was dying and moved into making the most of the time he had left. That spring day on the deck we talked about how to prepare for his last days—just eight short years after falling in love. One month later he took his last breath.

His ending is where this story begins. It's a story of beauty, where, in facing his own end, he taught many how to live. His death created a new beginning for me; unexpected and unwanted, but new nonetheless. It's a story about turning the loss of his death into gratitude for his life and for my own. It's a story about grief, written from within grief, where I found a place of gratitude I hadn't expected.

In the year before Michael died, I had been writing regularly. I wrote a blog about healing foods as our family navigated our way through his illness and treatment. The focus on nourishment supported us in many ways, and preparing healing food was something I could tangibly do to nourish us all physically. After his death, everything shifted. I came to know the meaning of nourishment from a whole new perspective. Despite the heaviness of grief, I needed to write down all that passed through my heart as the days unfolded. I wrote about what nourished me during that time—what truly nourished me. No longer the physical nourishment from food, but the deeper nourishment, that which tapped into the place inside that said, "Yes" to being alive. And that place for me was gratitude. A place of thanks when it seemed like there was nothing to feel thankful for. I knew that gratitude was nourishment, Divine nourishment, direct from my Source.

I know the concept of gratitude within grief may be hard to accept as genuine. Yet what I found over this last year was that instead of gratitude being something I talked myself into in order to feel better, it became a daily invitation to attune to what was present in the moment. Finding gratitude in the moment, even with the pain, became the key to continuing to choose to live.

At many points in my grieving and mourning process I have not felt gratitude. In this book, I share those darker times as well. I share them as a way of saying that the pain of grief has been, and continues to be, real for me. But beyond the pain have been different moments: those when someone made me laugh or the brilliance of a flower tuned me into the surrounding beauty. Each and every moment of a year has passed, filled with grief or filled with gratitude, and what flows in and out of all those moments is grace—the inexplicable awareness that there is something greater within these moments that weaves them into one larger tapestry of life.

At times while writing, I couldn't imagine feeling grateful so soon after his death. Yet I did, even many months later when I was still in the depths of mourning. I realize a sacredness can surround death which seems to make all things possible, even gratitude. It is a sacredness I remember from my years as a hospice nurse; walking into a home and feeling the space as if entering a magnificent cathedral. Irrespective of anything going on in the room, for me there was always a palpable luminescence.

I have such clear memories of the luminosity present with us during the time of his dying. The luminosity was real. Something was present. We were held in the sacredness of passage as clearly as the essence of a room changes right as a baby is born.

I sense the sacredness again now as this book comes to a finish.

In birth and death, everything changes. Whether from our own human and earthbound energetics of awe and wonder or whether something larger truly is holding us matters not.

I don't know which is true, but what matters to me is the remembering of the sacredness, the understanding that awe moves us to gratitude, and thus toward the process of living. In choosing to focus on gratitude, I moved to an understanding that there is a depth and breadth to life that is possible to touch in a way that informs our whole way of living—and as it turns out, our way of dying.

In retrospect, I could have written about life before Michael died, but I was too full of hope and too busy fighting to keep him here with us. It was after his death that I felt compelled to write, needed to write, in order to keep living in the days, weeks, and months following his death.

I'm also aware now, in having written about grief, that there are many books about people facing life-threatening illnesses, and yet very few that share what happens afterwards. In these books and movies about illness and death, it seems like everything ends when the lead character dies. The valiant effort and herculean struggles play out, and then it rolls to credits as if that's the end of the story. But then what? What happens the next morning, or over the next year? The afterwards isn't as dramatic, yet its potential for strength, grit, and triumph are just as strong. But these are so often hidden in a culture where death and grief are rarely discussed.

My writing about grief and gratitude is a response to that afterwards. It was written out of my own search for a roadmap. I wanted someone to tell me what it felt like from the inside. I wanted to know I was normal, that what I was feeling was okay, that I wasn't crazy. In the beginning, writing was what got me through the toughest times of grief. But as I wrote day after day, I began to see the results as something to share with others.

It is not my intention to share this book as a way to grieve, for I know not all grief is the same. I know we each have our own journey, outside of all the stereotypes and maps and theories and stages. I know we all have different relationships with those we are grieving for, whether it be a parent, sibling, spouse, or child. I also think we grieve similarly to the way we live. Our own beliefs, qualities, and characteristics create a unique experience for each of us as we face the inevitable human journey through loss.

I share my passage through this time as a way for others who are grieving to find solace in the commonalities we may share. I offer it also to those looking in from the outside to see how to support those they know who are in the depths of grief. It is often awkward and uncomfortable being around those who are grieving. It can be uncomfortable from both sides. And yet we won't escape death or grief. Every one of us will die and will experience people we love dying.

This book reflects my own journey through a year of grief. It was written in real time, and in order to honor the process and perspective from the inside of the grief experience, it has been edited very little and at times remains quite raw. The sharing of my journey is a way to support the conversation of grieving as being a normal experience we all walk through. Hopefully the journeys through grief which lay ahead can be more open, more shared, and with more companions, so that none of us ever has to feel alone in grief.

This is my story of learning to sing amidst the sadness, and learning, through the gift of grace, to find gratitude amidst the grief.

The First Days

MAY 28TH - 31ST 2012

"I didn't cry. I couldn't. I only breathed finally, my own breath without the automatic syncing to his ragged breathing—and I knew that his suffering was finally over. What I am beginning to know only now, is that for those of us who are left behind, our journey through a new kind of suffering has only just begun."

Monday, Day One

I'm not sure how to meet this morning after Michael's death, but I do know I am grateful for my urge to be writing. I know writing calms my emotions, and that writing helps me look at this experience as real and worth sharing. It seems odd to me that today, of all days, is the day when my writing feels more inspired than it has in all my years of putting words to the page. I suppose I need something to fill the emptiness, the quiet space where his breath used to be.

I want to share so much about the last few days, the pain and the beauty of the days leading up to his death, and the surreal nature of today. After all we have been through, it feels strange to be up and moving around and acting as if life is still normal in some way. I find myself getting up out of bed, making tea, practicing yoga, feeding our dog, and doing all the other early morning quiet things I used to do each day. It feels odd to still be living, to have this world to come back to after being day-in and day-out in the presence of someone who is was dying. It was as if I too was dying, and I suppose in a way there is a part of me that has died to this world and will never see it the same again. Everything has changed. My husband has died, and in response, I get up the morning after and make tea.

I think Lucas, at the tender age of six, had it right when he said this morning, when I asked him how he was feeling, "It feels like I should be asking a question, and it makes me feel crazy." He twirled his finger around his ear and bobbled his head to communicate that he too felt off balance and unstable. Perhaps like a cartoon character that has just has his head whacked and can't quite seem to recover. Off-balance is an understatement, and I can only imagine what he is feeling on this day after his father has died.

This morning we sat snuggling and talking about grief. I was talking to him, in a very knowledgeable parental voice, about how the way to grieve is to feel exactly what you are feeling. I told him that grief might be expressed as feeling sad, happy, angry, or peaceful. I wanted him to understand that whatever he was feeling was okay. As it turns out, grief for him feels crazy. All I could say was "Me too, sweetie, me too." How could we be feeling anything else?

Crazy seems like the only logical feeling for us to be experiencing as we ride the entire range of human emotions from minute to minute, enduring this fluctuation for hours on end. It's only been a day, and I'm already overwhelmed as the questions come rushing in as to what my future will look like. I wonder all at once—while feeling nearly nothing—what it means to be a mother raising a son, a young widow, or a grieving spouse. They are all labels and have nothing to do with me. I know it's just another striving for definition, comfort, or security. A grasping for some template for how I am now supposed to feel, act, survive, or present myself to the world.

I'm done with grasping. We, my sweet Michael and I, have been grasping for the last year and a half. At first we grasped for a cure, and then when that wasn't possible, we grasped for a graceful death. Neither happened the way we wanted.

And yet, I somehow know it was all perfect in its own way. And I can't now, after his death, grieve or live according to some expectation.

Yesterday was not how I imagined it, or how I expected it, but how could I ever imagine his last breath or the way in which my whole body tingled as he left this earthly plane? Or how could I imagine bathing and dressing his body after he died? I didn't imagine it, I suppose, because in the days preceding his death, I was busy doing all sorts of other things I never thought I would have to do as I cared for him. I went through the last month of his life simply doing what was in front of me. There truly wasn't time or room for any thinking or contemplating about what would come next, simply because the suffering in the current moment was too overwhelming to possibly let in any new information of what might happen in the future.

I never could have imagined how it would end; how I would sit next to his bed, with his pain finally under control after days of struggle, and simply be doing nothing particularly special to mark the moment when his last breath finally came. It had been too long, and we had tried so hard to anticipate and somehow prepare for his last moment. We didn't know how quickly his condition would deteriorate, how uncontrolled his symptoms would be, and how much care he would need in his last days. My stepson, Leit, moved in with us to help, and my mom stayed as well to care for Lucas. We all wanted to follow his wishes to die at home with hospice care, and we did the best we could to support a peaceful transition and ease his suffering. We had the music thanatology harpist from hospice with us to gently ease him on his journey. We played meditations for the dying. We meditated next to him for hours, and we found music to facilitate a graceful passage.

But in the end, I was simply sitting next to him, quietly listening to his breathing, reading something mindless and acutely aware that this could go on for moments or for days. And then there was a subtle shift, almost imperceptible, in which I knew he was dying. And one breath later he was gone.

My body tingled, and then a wisp of feeling, like the softness of wind, brushed against my face, and there was stillness deeper than I can ever explain. He was gone, and all that remained was peace.

I didn't cry. I couldn't. I only breathed—finally, my own breath without the automatic syncing to his ragged breathing—and I knew that his suffering was finally over. What I am beginning to know only now, is that for those of us who are left behind, our journey through a new kind of suffering has only just begun.

I am now in a strange world of the unknown. My life that was once clear is now filled with uncertainty.

Everything feels awkward and unanticipated in the wake of his death. I had all of my energy focused on his transition, with no forethought as to what I might need to do next.

I wanted to feel like I knew exactly what to do with his body after he passed, that all my years of hospice training would make it simple and obvious. I know the basics, and that I needed to call the mortuary at some point. I knew I could take whatever time I needed to be with him after he died. Beyond that, I hadn't made a plan. I had simply been surviving for the last two weeks, sleeplessly trying to manage the pain, breathlessness, anxiety, and confusion that marked the final days of his illness. When the stillness finally came, I didn't know what to do. There was no crisis or connection to lean into, there was simply quiet. Michael and I had talked about what he wanted for his body in general, but we never talked about what to do right after he died. Perhaps that was too painful to consider, and too unimaginable with him still there with me.

As it was, my mom, Leit, and I did what seemed right. We found music that wasn't too sad or too upbeat, a washcloth, some scented oil, and his favorite clothes, and we tried our best to pay respects to the body that had carried his soul on this earth. I'd like to think we completed the ritual of caring for his body in the way he would have wanted, but the truth is we just did the best we knew how, and it felt good to be doing something in the empty space that hung around us like a heavy cloth.

Later, when Lucas came home from our neighbor's house, I had to tell him his daddy had died. I expected to reread him one of the books we had bought about death and remind him again how bodies look after people die. I had been talking about Michael's death with him for weeks, preparing him as best I knew how. I told him all about what Michael's body might look like and what it means when a person has died. We did everything the books told us to, and yet I wanted to take more time and to hold him. I wanted desperately to know, as a mother, what to do in this situation that seemed so incredibly impossible and incongruent to be telling my six-year-old.

Lucas had said goodbye to Michael that morning, so when I told him Michael had died, I think I expected him to cry and be sad and have questions. I thought we would have some time to prepare. But instead, he ran upstairs ahead of me without wanting to talk at all. I felt like it was all wrong and out of control and that there must be some perfect way to prepare your child to see a loved one's body. But there wasn't; there was only what happened.

Lucas went into the bedroom and saw Michael and asked questions about why he looked so different. He was clearly more aware than I was that Michael's body was simply now a body. We held each other and then lit some incense next to the photo of Michael by the bed. He looked at the incense and the candles for a long time, and then he said he wanted to watch *Spider-Man*.

So I did what I never imagined a grieving wife would do after her husband dies: I watched *Spider-Man*.

I watched *Spider-Man*, and I held our little boy, and I breathed in and breathed out, and that was how it went the first day.

Tuesday, Day Two

This morning I am grateful for my yoga practice, as well as for the previous fifteen years of daily practice that makes the routine as automatic as brushing my teeth in the morning. I am grateful for all the small efforts I made over the years to create my habits of yoga, meditation, breathing, and walking in nature. These habits nourish and feed me, and are now so natural that I hardly notice I'm making a wise choice by doing them. My body has been programmed to know that if I do yoga, if I breathe, then I will feel alive. And today I need the programming to be intact, as I cannot muster any feeling of aliveness on my own.

In my yoga practice this morning there was the breath, the asana, a slight awakening of energy in my body, and there were tears. Even after so many years of yoga, I still do a relatively beginning practice. I have often aspired to do more, but the simplicity itself is what opens my body, and on this day it opens my emotions. Yoga makes me feel alive. It helps me realize it's not the asana but the act of opening each day to that which is present in the moment. Breathing consciously as I move through the poses is a way of staying more alive, aware, and awake in this world. No more, no less. Today I am grateful my yoga is a lifeline. I breathe in, breathe out, move my body, and know that I am indeed alive despite the haze of trauma that surrounds me.Before I started my morning's practice I put on music, and, just as has happened twice since

Michael died, the song that automatically played was a chant by the singer Snatam Kaur called "Ong Namo." As I listened to this song, more tears and more gratitude flowed forward. For this was the song that I sang to him the day before he died, as I held him in bed and cradled his heart in the only position that eased the pain. I had heard and chanted that song a thousand times the past few years, and in that moment, holding him, I knew it was the song to sing quietly in his ear. I knew the words were sacred, but only later did I come to know that they translated to: "I call on Divine Wisdom." Indeed, in that moment, that was the only wisdom available that would help either one of us through the journey.

In this memory I am also grateful for the angel, Therese Schroeder-Sheker, whose teachings opened me to the field of Music Thanatology, which gave me guidance in that moment of holding him before he died. Over fifteen years ago, when I was in nursing school, I read an article of hers. The article described her working as an aide in a nursing home and coming across a man dying alone in his room. Her intuition encouraged her to climb into bed with him, and to cradle and sing to him until he died. So when Michael was suffering and there was nothing else to offer but my own comfort, I remembered the wisdom she shared. I knew to get into bed behind him while we waited for the hospice physician to arrive, and to cradle his heart and sing to him.

As I held him, the words of "Ong Namo" enfolded us, and as I remember back to those moments, I am grateful for what came through me to ease his pain; to realize that calling on Divine Wisdom in that moment was truly the only way to peace. I didn't "think" to do this, just as I didn't "think" to do yoga this morning; I simply listened to that which came automatically. I'm grateful for the wisdom inside me that knew how to soothe when I couldn't think my way to soothing, and for the body wisdom of yoga that keeps me alive in my body when I don't feel aliveness.

May this wisdom nourish me in the days to come.

Wednesday, Day Three

I have to admit that I am stunned at how much comes forward each day to be grateful for in the midst of so much pain. I feel that in some way the inspiration to be writing and the attention to gratitude that lifts me from my grief are gifts that have come from having touched the veil between life and death so closely with Michael. I feel held in a cloak of loving, as so many beautiful souls come forward to support us as we respond to the reality of Michael's death.

I've been overwhelmed with details in the three short days since his passing. There are so many phone calls to make, so much paperwork to attend to and planning to be done, and it all feels so foreign after the days of being isolated, insulated, and completely focused on attending to his care and passage into death. I'm bombarded by everything needing my input, and I'm beginning to realize the only way through is to accept help. Gratefully, the help is right here, waiting for me.

As I reach out for this help, I find that the beauty of what is offered astounding. I just got off the phone with the director of the Portland Peace Choir that I've been singing with for the last two years. She offered to put together the music for Michael's memorial service, and I am incredibly grateful. I'm grateful for the music, but also for the wisdom she shared. She told me her sister had lost her husband to cancer four years ago. After his death, her sister remarked that she wished she could skip ahead six months so she wouldn't have to experience such grief. I wish that for myself as well and verbalized it with her tonight; the feeling of just wanting the logistics, the pain, the transitions, all the firsts without Michael, to be complete so I can feel some distance from the grief. But then I also realized that if I don't feel each moment now, I'll be numb to the amazing amount of support and love that's here and present for me. This is so hard, and yet in the midst of it all, I am seeing the depth of love expressed by those around me as I walk through this time.

I am also grateful for the beauty and spaciousness of the Oregon coast. Yesterday we all piled into the car, Lucas, Leit, my mom, my sister, and I, and drove an hour out to the beach just to be away from the intense reminders of the last month. We needed space from the pressure of so many people wanting to see us, talk with us, and find out the details for the memorial service.

As it turned out, we planned the service along the way. All five of us, together in the car, with nothing to do but think about what would be simple, elegant, and honoring of Michael. The time was perfect for us to talk, and then we arrived at the coast, on a beautiful expanse of pristine beach on a late spring weekday without another soul in sight. We built sandcastles, filled our lungs with clear ocean air, played in the waves, and watched our dog, Alta, run joyously free on the beach. We let all the intensity of the last months breathe for a couple of hours. I played with Lucas, running from the waves, writing love notes to each other with our toes in the sand, and re-membering what it felt like to be open and happy for a few moments.

Nothing had changed when we got home. We were all exhausted, and grief hung round the house with the thick memories of the previous days of anguish and loss. We had made a plan, but there were still a million things to do. But we were buoyed by the beach and by the time taken to remember what it feels like to live in the midst of a time of dying. We needed the air and the energy of play, and I am grateful for the accessibility of the beach and our wisdom to let go and open into movement and space.

Thursday, Day Four

Gratitude was harder to come by today. I'm tired, and I just want to be in bed and cry. The world going on outside seems strange, as if it too should be stunned and disoriented by Michael's death. So many people reaching out, and I just want to be alone. Everything seems to make my heart ache.

I want Sunday to be over. I want the service to be out of the way and all the busyness of preparation to be done and the visitors to have gone home. And yet I know all too well the immeasurable emptiness that looms ahead. I know deep inside there is nothing that can make the ache easier—busy or not busy, I will grieve.

So I'll start small today with the gratitude.

I'm grateful for the compassion of the funeral home director, who took the time to save out the small heart-shaped stone that I put in Michael's pocket after he died. I had told her about it, and she found it for me and put it on top of the container that held his ashes.

I'm grateful for the sun being out today and the feel of its warmth on my face as I took a drink of water after walking Alta at the park.

I'm grateful for my son's first grade teacher, who spent all yesterday afternoon with the kids in Lucas's class making cards for him for when he returns to school.

I'm grateful for my sister being here, walking beside me through all of this, and thinking clearly when I can't seem to track well.

I'm tired and everything aches, but I'm grateful that I'm writing and able to stay clear enough to keep going; to somehow imagine that this writing is a way toward something that will feel fulfilling in the future.

I am somehow grateful.

June

"I need to find my own compass, to discover the place within that trusts the wisdom in the silence will reveal the next step ~ or help me merely get to the next moment."

Friday, June 1st

Immense gratitude at a time with so much grief feels like a miracle, and yet gratitude is what I experienced today. In between tears and tiredness, I let myself feel the beauty of what a circle of strong women can do together.

After much consideration of venues, we are having Michael's service in the backyard here at the house. My mom, sister, Leit, and I created a task list a mile long and we each had chosen things to complete before Sunday. One of my choices was to work outside, and a dear old friend asked today if she could come and help. I told her it would be great to have some help with the weeds in the yard. She immediately took the day off from work and showed up with gardening clothes and a tender smile.

Another friend who flew up from California for the service also asked if she could come by for the day to help. And then, by chance, yet one more friend heard I was working in the yard and decided to put on her gardening clothes and come on over.

What happened next was a miracle. My aspirations of having the weeds pulled around the yard's edges turned in a matter of hours to a landscaping transformation. It went from a decent backyard to a beautiful setting with blooming plants and gorgeous color; a place in which to remember my beloved on Sunday.

Most importantly during that time, I was able to cry and laugh with three dear friends. I let myself be held, I let myself cry, and I let myself be present to the moments of gratitude that emerged with each touch of the soil.

I could have stayed in bed, let everyone else do the work, but I needed to put the energy of grief somewhere. And I missed my friends. I was tired of grieving, of feeling the pain of illness and death, and so the act of putting my hands in the soil with people who love me was the one thing that made sense.

Saturday, June 2nd

There is a quiet softness to the air this evening, here in our home. I went outside after putting Lucas to bed and said a small prayer to Michael about having the service in the backyard. I don't know if he could hear me, but I asked him to bless us and to bless the service for him tomorrow; to hold a space of loving light for all of us to feel clear and open to the Divinity of whatever unfolds. I've been so worried about all the things that might go awry: having too many people, it raining, the yard not being ready, not enough food...the list of worries goes on and on. Yet I realize that underneath all those worries is the intense pain of doing this all for him, but without him here. He was such a wonderful host, and it feels strange to be planning and prepping for people to be with us here in our home without him.

I needed to feel him outside with me tonight, to sense his presence, even if just in my heart. The numbness has been good at getting me through these last few days, and for that I am thankful. Yet as time goes on, I feel the anesthetizing salve of shock and denial wearing off. I feel tender and alone in the midst of so many people trying to provide comfort.

I miss him.

Earlier today I went into his closet, away from all the well-meaning friends downstairs, because I just needed to feel him. I found his bathrobe, still hanging on the hook, and was so incredibly relieved that it still smelled like him. I breathed it in and sobbed.

I'm sad that he isn't here for this celebration of his life, but mostly I'm sad that he isn't here for me. I feel the emptiness in our room, in our home, and the hardest thing about it all is that I can't feel him. I can't find any sense of anything about him other than this vast emptiness where his warmth used to be. I want to know that he's here, but when I tune in all I feel is hurt and pain.

Until tonight.

When I went outside, alone and quiet. For just a brief second, I could sense him in the dark with me. Not right next to me, as he would have been, but out there somewhere; a feeling, a sense, an awareness of him watching and witnessing. His warmth was there, in an all-knowing, observing kind of way that couldn't participate—maybe didn't even have the desire to participate—but was still incredibly loving. In that brief moment of awareness I felt my longing for him, my longing for him to be with me in a way that was more palpable, more real, more alive.

I want to feel his aliveness, and yet as I write this, I remember the promise I made to him just after he died. I promised I wouldn't try to pull him back with the depth of my emotion—that I would be strong for him. And in that moment outside tonight, in my awareness of him in my mind's eye, I saw and heard him laugh, knowing there was no possible way for me to pull him back. Instead, I could be as emotional as I needed to be, and he would be strong for me on the other side of the veil.

I have been strong for him for such a long time. I cared for him with all the grace and courage I could bring forward. Now he was telling me to lean on him and to let him be strong for me. So I lift my heart up tonight—a grateful heart for this memory of my promise after his passing—and I let myself grieve all the loss and all the pain; knowing that he is standing strong on the other side, holding with a grace much larger than my human abilities; knowing that in some way tomorrow will go smoothly, and he will be there in some form, holding in the vastness of loving grace.

Sunday, June 3rd - Michael's Service

So many things came forward to find gratitude in today. Everything easily flowed together for Michael's service through the many loving hands that worked to make it happen. Our ministerial friends, Connie and John, officiated elegantly. The Peace Choir sang a prayer just as the sun opened into the sky, and I felt a glimpse of ascension as its rays filtered through the pines and held us in sacred space. So many hearts touched mine today in a way that made me begin to believe that we truly will be held in a loving community, and people will be here for us in the days, weeks, and months ahead.

There was also a weird moment. At one stage, I flashed back to what it felt like at our wedding. So many people wanted to say something to me, to touch in and make contact. Yet now it felt strange, as if I was the hostess but didn't have anything to say to anyone. I know they were paying their respects, and it was important to them to speak with me. It also felt vulnerable to be hugged by people who seemed unaware that they were pouring their own grief into me instead of providing comfort. I was grateful people came, and yet I felt oddly on display and obligated to be gracious at a time when I seriously couldn't feel anything.

Afterwards, a few people stayed: family and close friends, people who had come from out of town. A good friend brought a bottle of wine, and that was helpful in the communion of it, and in the symbolic nature of acknowledging that it was time to let go a bit, to let tears flow, to be held close.

I'm grateful that my closest friends knew not to leave right away, while the aftereffects of the service were still reverberating through the backyard. They knew to stay, to help me with the tearful goodbyes to friends who had come from afar. They stayed long enough for me to transition to bed and put this day behind me, with all of its grace and all of its pain. To be complete.

Monday, June 4th

I'm grateful to have made it through the day, and to have ended it by mustering enough energy to put my feet in the tub while my sweet little boy took a bath. I've been hurting all day, my heart and my bones, and I feel, deep in my core, the loss that surrounds me throughout our home.

I feel like I spin off-kilter with every tiny decision or request of me.

I feel like hiding.

I don't even look at my phone to see who is calling.

I am so grateful for my friends, and yet even though they check on me so sweetly and consistently, they seem worlds away. I can't bring myself to answer the phone or call back. I don't want to talk about how I feel. It already hurts so badly.

I am grateful for the wisdom today to have listened to my heart and my body and to have turned inside; to have done only what was absolutely required to take care of Lucas, who desperately needs me right now; and to soften a bit so I can open to myself and my own emotions.

I know I need to find my own compass on this journey; to discover the place inside that can listen into the silence and reveal the next step—or help me merely get to the next moment. I am grateful for the space and quiet that my mother and sister provided for me today, the way they acted as a buffer between me and a world that wants my participation and yet seems so strangely far away.

Tuesday, June 5th

Today I'm grateful for my friends, who keep showing up even as I shut down. I'm grateful for all the kind people who helped me on the phone today. I'm deeply touched by condolences from people who don't even know me. As I struggled with one of too many paperwork details, complete strangers not only assisted me, but expressed a level of compassion that brought me to tears.

Not that it's challenging to bring me to tears these days. The numbness has worn off and I am overwhelmed and left with a constant stream of tears.

But I'm grateful I was able to get a few things done today. I'm even thinking I may be able to sort through enough financial paperwork to find that I'll be able to stay in the house another year instead of having to consider moving in the next couple of months. Everyone tells me not to make any big decisions in the first six months to a year, and yet I don't think anyone realizes that the loss of a spouse, the loss of a life partner, brings forward in every realm a whole cascade of big decisions that feel immediate and pressing.

I'm grateful for the time Michael and I spent going over finances before he died.

I'm grateful that all our accounts are joint accounts.

I'm grateful that I know how to mow the lawn.

I'm grateful that Lucas is still in school for another week, so that I have time to think amidst the waves of grief.

I want to find within me the space to trust that it's okay to be silent and to sit in that silence and trust there will be guidance. There's a part of me that's afraid to stop moving, afraid that I will either be overtaken by grief, or worse, afraid there will be a silence devoid of faith. I want to trust in my faith. And so tomorrow, I will start again. I will get up again and move through the day, and I suppose for now that is enough faith; enough of a showing to trust that the silence and the quiet and the reflection that has steadied me through the years is actually present, working behind the scenes to keep me moving through the days that lie ahead.

Wednesday, June 6th

Earlier, I talked with my mom about writing each night. I told her how the emptiness I find when I come up to bed is so heavy that it seems to be the perfect time to write about gratitude. The writing keeps me from falling into the void of sadness as I go up to our room, so full of memories. I write until I'm too tired to think and then I simply fall asleep. I miss him so desperately at night— the time in which we were always together.

Michael and I had this funny habit of not wanting to go to bed when the other person was still up. If one of us was tired, the other one would either go to bed and read, or the one who was tired would give in to the lure of a rare evening movie after Lucas was asleep. I don't know why, but it seemed important to him that we go to bed at the same time, and I have to admit it was comforting. He and I would settle into our bed, the house quiet and dark, and we'd float into dreams inside the beautiful wooden bedframe he built a couple of years ago.

He was an amazing woodworker. He built in a style we called Asian arts and craft that has a soft yet sturdy look to it. His work is so solid, as if nothing that was made by his hands could ever crumble or break. I feel safe in this bed, even without his presence.

Maybe I still feel safe because he taught me how to love myself as much as he loved me. Maybe all the fears I had before I knew him were simply my own fears of inadequacy. Being loved by him made me a stronger person;

the kind of person, I suppose, who can write in bed when I'm lonely, or the kind of person who can see gratitude when the world is falling apart around me. I don't know why this is working, but it seems to be. This time of day is made easier through writing, even when the grief seems to be leaking into every other corner of my life. The writing helps, and I'm grateful for the evening respite.

As I reflect on today, I remember most clearly the trip I took to the grocery store. I haven't been out much since his death, and it's taking me time to be comfortable going into the world. So today, for the first time, I went to the grocery store. And as I chose a cart at the door I started to shake. Memories of being there with him flooded through me. Memories of how normal it would have been to pick out some kale together for dinner. Every aisle reminded me of him. His favorite foods haunted me as I tried to just finish up my list and check out.

I didn't expect to feel so much at the grocery store. I didn't expect to cry at the grocery store. Yet I see how the times when I least expect my emotions are the times when they come the strongest. I am grateful to have one more "first time without Michael" out of the way, and I'm grateful to recognize the process as it unfolds and trust myself to ride the waves of grief and not care who sees me cry.

Thursday, June 7th

I'm grateful that it rained today. When I took Alta for a walk, the park was empty and I could let myself open to whatever emotions came forward. The gray skies and heavy rain protected me and I could be alone while still being out in the world. I feel incredibly vulnerable, and although at times I can be out and doing normal things, there's an underlying unsteadiness within it all.

I spoke to a dear friend this afternoon, a friend who is also a therapist, and although she was speaking with me as a friend, her comforting words gave permission for all of the built-up feelings of the day to tumble out in deep sobs. I realized, in crying, the importance of being heard and held in grief by someone, even if only over the phone. I have cried on my own, and I have had tears well up with others, but today was the first time I let the grief come forward in more than a trickle, and there she was, so carefully holding me on the other end of the line. "That's right, let it come forward." In that moment, I was so grateful for being heard.

I'm aware there is a part of me that's hiding the grief.

Shame?

Guilt?

Responding to the awkwardness of so many who don't know what to say?

These seem like such strange emotions to be having. Yet I feel separate and alone, as if I'm marked by my grief as being different; someone to avoid. In that vein,

I realize how grateful I am for the friends who are willing to show up and be present at this time. I have such an urge to just pack up and move, take a huge road trip or find some new magical place to live where no one will know what happened or look at us with the sadness of what is missing.

I know the grief would follow me. I know that even if I wanted to, I couldn't get it together to sell the house and pack our things. I can barely pack a lunch. I guess there's a blessing in lack of function, some mechanism that protects us from making overly bold moves. So I will take each day, each hour, and at times each moment, as it comes. I will do my best not to think too far ahead. Tomorrow I will pack lunch for my son, and we will live another day of learning how to find our way in this new life.

Friday, June 8th

Tonight I'm grateful for yellow poppies and loving neighbors.

Earlier today, my next-door neighbors invited all the kids on the block over for a movie so the other parents could enjoy a date night or early dinner. Lucas really wanted to be with the kids, so I walked him over even though it felt awkward for me to not have anywhere to go. I navigated my way through the social discomfort, feeling the pain of my aloneness as I watched the other couples dash off together. I didn't want to just head back home, so I decided to go for a drive. In the car, I'm able to remember Michael more clearly. Listening to his music helps me connect to him, and the open sky a few minutes away from the city allows space in my head for memories of our amazing road trips.

At first, when I started to drive, it was excruciating to be alone in the car, headed out to nowhere without Michael. The music didn't help; it just made me sad. But then I drove out by the horse barn where I used to volunteer, and as I turned a corner, the whole roadside came ablaze with blooming yellow poppies. Both sides of the road were full of the bright flowers with the road just a narrow strip of blacktop between the swaths of yellow. I stopped to pick a handful, remembering how I brought some home for Michael after my walks when he was so sick that he couldn't get out of bed. I remembered how happy they made him.

It's the little things that make me smile these days, like believing those yellow poppies were some kind of sign. A sign that in some impossible-to-know way, he's still here, creating roadside displays of blossoming wildflowers. I know that the flowers probably bloom there every spring. I might have even driven past them before, but I noticed them tonight when I needed something to hold onto. The poppies reminded me of Michael and of a poem that I first heard after a good friend died. Written by Nancy Wood, it's called "Hold On to What is Good," and it touches my heart as deeply now as it did then:

Hold on to what is good
even if it is
a handful of earth.
Hold on to what you believe
even if it is
a tree which stands by itself.
Hold on to what you must do
even if it is
a long way from here.
Hold on to life even when
it is easier letting go.
Hold on to my hand even when
I have gone away from you.
*   - Nancy Wood*

The yellow poppies reminded me of that poem tonight, as did the view over the rolling hills from the top of the ridge above the horse barn. The poppies gave me something to hold onto, something real, right here in my life, more than a memory; a tangible thing to link me to his life. I miss him terribly, and there are times when I can't believe he is gone.

I was able to quiet my mind enough to talk with him out there, standing alone up on the ridge, the warm fleece of his jacket pulled up to my chin against the scattered drops of rain. I asked him how to move forward, how I would know what to do from here. I was quiet enough to ask, but I guess not quiet enough to hear the answer. Perhaps that will come later, or maybe not at all. But with a vase full of poppies by my bedside, I will be happier in the morning. They will be the first thing I see. They will be something to hold onto in this living, something to help me to remember the preciousness of what I once held in my hands, and the preciousness of what remains to believe in.

Saturday, June 9th

I am grateful for my son's bright blue eyes and joyful smile. I am grateful that even in the midst of grief, I can still meet him in that place of light and happiness that most six-year-olds embody.

Today we were waiting to meet a friend who had invited us out to a movie. We were early and I was barely holding it together, wondering how I was going to get through the amount of time a movie required me to be in public. I was desperate for a distraction, and so I challenged Lucas to our favorite game of "Make Me Laugh." To play, one person makes funny faces and noises until the other person laughs and then the roles switch. Lucas's laugh - is contagious, and it makes his eyes sparkle with life. I found myself in a better mood within minutes.

I am grateful to be his mom. I am grateful that he will still hold my hand at times. I am grateful for his lightheartedness and his thoughtfulness.

The truth is, I get overwhelmed every single day when I think about how to parent him on my own. I worry what it will be like for him not to have his dad, and yet I see how this worry puts the same labels on him that I am trying so hard not to put on myself. I want to resist the urge to associate with the cultural norms, the labels, the roles, and mostly any expectation for how he should act or experience his life because his father died. I don't want it to be something wrong or terrible that happened to him, but instead be a blessing to have had Michael in his life at all.

At the memorial service, Lucas's first grade teacher came up and looked me clearly in the eye. She acknowledged our loss, but also the remarkable miracle that I had the time I did with Michael. I am grateful, even in the midst of grief, to remember the magic and the wonder and the love that filled our eight years together. I got it that not everyone has the opportunity to truly love and be loved in a relationship. I get it that I should feel lucky. I still want him back.

Sunday, June 10th

Tonight I am tremendously grateful for my dear friend, Inge. We have known each other for over twenty years, and I have to say there's something incredibly purposeful about the love of an enduring friendship. Over the years, we've been through just about everything together: job changes, moves, kids, marriage, parents dying, crises and joys of all sorts. Now, of course, she is here for me through Michael's death and my grieving. She promised last week that she would stay close, and it wasn't more than a day or two before she invited us over for dinner.

I was so blessed this evening to hear our children laughing and to be held in a space of loving. There was just the right amount of acknowledgment of Michael's absence while still being present to the beauty that unfolded in our families being together.

I have to admit I find it hard to be with other families, yet at the same time I so clearly want friends to hold Lucas and I close and include us in activities and dinners. The emptiness is more acute when viewed against the backdrop of another family—a vague reminder of when I was single and would be included with married couples, yet not feel completely a part of things. I know it is my fear of isolation coming through, and any perception I have of us being separate is an illusion. My friends are making such an effort to include us, and I know I am gracefully supported. Instead of being afraid that it will suddenly stop when everyone gets back to their busy lives, I want to trust that we truly are part of a community of loving. And I know that being part of a community of loving starts with me being loving; with myself, our son, our friends, and the incredible village of friends surrounding us with love and support. It is my intention to trust in the love instead of aloneness.

Monday, June 11th

I am grateful for the sweet taste of margaritas on a warm spring evening. I am grateful for kids being able to run in the yard barefoot and dream of late summer nights when the last days of school are finally over. I am grateful that we were not alone tonight and instead were wrapped again in the loving arms of one of our community of families.

I am touched by and grateful for my friends' husbands and how they so quietly, strongly, and elegantly support their wives in supporting me. I hadn't thought of how it would be to spend time with our friends without Michael. He so perfectly fit in everywhere we went, that to go somewhere without him and wonder how to interact socially feels strange. I'm seeing strength in these men, who I've known and yet not known because they were always interacting with Michael. Now here they are, present and supportive, and yet not obtrusively acting out of character when they interact with me. They are simply themselves. And they are giving their wives, my women friends, a beautiful space in which to be with me. They are giving me room to be vulnerable without making it a huge crisis that I might be crying on the porch while they play foursquare with the kids in the yard.

These last couple of nights spent with other families, give me hope that we will not be lost in the mix of social taboos. I see how much fear I have about being left out or left behind, and I am aware of the work I need to do with this myself so as to not create that illusion for Lucas. We are well loved and we are going to be held by our community.

I'm also grateful for the quiet today. I was alone for the first time in months and I was okay. I've been so afraid of being alone, of completely breaking down and falling off the face of the earth. I thought I would cry and not be able to stop if I ever faced the acuity of my aloneness. Instead, I was relieved to fall into my own familiar rhythm of doing things around the house. I wasn't terribly functional, but I found that I could trust myself to be stable as I attempted some efforts at normalcy in the quiet space of our home.

The beautiful part of being alone was that I felt like I could be fully authentic to what I needed in each moment. I am so grateful for the support of family and friends, and yet the freedom of simply being with my own energy today felt incredibly liberating. My direction for the day was less confusing. I'm not saying that I was engaged in anything purposeful or that what needed to be done got done, but I did feel clear and able to focus. I will be grateful for the help of family when Lucas is out of school for the summer, but today also gave me hope that come fall, and perhaps even sooner, I will be able to find a new sense of normal and my own direction in the world.

Tuesday, June 12th

I am grateful for the power and grace available through authentic self-forgiveness.

I woke again at three in the morning, unable to sleep, with the images of the last few days of Michael's life replaying in my head. I know I did my best caring for him, yet I still wonder if there was something I could have done to make him more comfortable; that maybe I could have been more patient or kind with him when I was so tired from being up for days on end that I could barely stand.

And as those images and scenarios ran through my head, I began to forgive myself: for judging myself in those last days; for judging my feelings of impatience, frustration, fatigue, helplessness, anger; for judging my overwhelming pain. I cried and cried with the relief of my own forgiveness. I had thought I needed something external to tell me I had done enough, but it was truly what I was holding against myself that tortured me with images at night.

I forgave myself. And fell asleep. And dreamed. In those dreams, I realized a part of me feels so alone and afraid without Michael. It's as if we had been on a life raft together, getting through a terrible storm, but when the seas settled I found myself alone and adrift in a vast ocean. I don't know how to live without him here, but I feel like I'm supposed to be doing something, meeting some expectation, behaving a certain way when all I want is to find my own bearings and regain balance within myself. I lost my center in those last days and during the days of grief and paperwork and planning that followed.

A part of me desperately needs silence right now and it's bumping against a whole community full of people who want to support me. And now I realize it's my own self denying the silence and pushing me out into the world before I'm ready, when I truly want to just curl up and stay in bed and maybe get up for a bath or a cup of tea. Everyone wants to know if I'm okay, and in reality I haven't given myself time to figure out the answer to that particular question.

Yet even as I write these words, I know I'm going to be okay. For now, and perhaps even a year from now, whatever I am doing to move toward healing is valid. It may be that some days I will be completely floored by the grief, and I need to somehow make that acceptable within my own consciousness. I have been so busy doing things and trying to keep Lucas moving and entertained that I myself have been lost in the busyness of hiding from the grief. Yet I need to accept that this is a part of the journey as well.

I found this out most clearly today when I went to visit the horses at the barn where I volunteered last year. I hadn't seen them in months, and yet it was as if they could read everything that had happened in our time apart.

As I walked each one out to pasture, the horses reflected to me that my tenderness is what is most present in my field of energy. Over the past year these horses so clearly taught me about the perception they're capable of, and today they reflected a quiet tenderness that opened my heart to the depth of my feelings. Even the feisty ones were completely quiet for me as I put on their rain blankets and halters. They all held in complete stillness. Walking out to the pasture, they were calm and affectionate. They reflected my own tenderness, and mirrored to me a way to be with myself that up until then I hadn't been able to see. They mirrored with their energy gentleness, calmness, evenness, and a quiet steadiness that gave me room to feel without being overwhelmed. These creatures of great sensitivity have taught me so much about myself. Today they taught me about the gentleness with which grief can be held.

Wednesday, June 13th

Michael didn't give me advice very often. We had a relationship where advice just seemed odd and disconnected from our base of communication. If one of us was in a quandary or upset with some injustice in the world, then the best thing for the other to do (and I'm not saying we always did this) was to be present, listen thoughtfully, hold back the screaming throngs of advice givers in our head, and wait for the other person to come to their own conclusion.

We usually came to the same conclusions anyway, so in the end we avoided the responsibility of giving advice or making the decision for the other person. Most of all, and most importantly, we felt heard. It worked well, and it is serving me well now in trusting that I can make good decisions even while being overwhelmed at so many macro levels by things that need attending to in the wake of Michael's death.

He didn't give me advice very often, so when he did I knew to listen. Which is why I so clearly remember some advice that he did give me. Before he died, perhaps in the last week or so, he advised me to surround myself with a circle of wise women and trust that they could hold anything that would come up for me. Turns out he was right.

I know I may sound gender-biased here, and I know wise men are present for me now and will be along the way. But I think Michael knew that right now I would be feeling incredibly vulnerable and insecure without his physical presence. Insecure seems like such a strange word to describe myself, but I do feel insecure and unsure of so many things. In this insecurity, I am able to be more vulnerable with women. It's easier with a woman to say that I'm an absolute emotional mess and feel like a complete idiot for not understanding everything I think I should be understanding right now, and how our house and my ability to care for our son depends upon that understanding.

So I have surrounded myself with wise women and I am grateful. I'm grateful, of course, for the obvious wise women around me: my mother, sister, close friends, and mentors. Yet today, what I glimpsed at every turn, is that from this conscious decision to call in women-wisdom, I seem to have called forward an awe-inspiring legion.

The first woman who completely surprised me today in her candid, compassionate, and clear support, was the estate lawyer a friend had referred me to. Our friend said she was a good and compassionate lawyer, and he thought I might be more comfortable working with a woman. He was right. She was perfect. The most amazing thing about her was that she expected and navigated my emotions as if they were the most normal expressions she had ever seen. I hadn't expected to be emotional, but had to blink back tears several times during our meeting. After each time it looked like I might cry, she would give me a moment to regain my composure before steering me back to the tasks at hand. She didn't make me feel like my tears were wrong, but rather par for the course. I left her office feeling confident that I could be an emotional wreck *and* still understand the ins and outs of estate taxes and mortgages.

The second woman who took me by surprise today was the children's social worker at hospice. I called to talk with her about Lucas, wanting to make sure I'm providing him with the support he needs to navigate this loss in his six-year-old way. She reassured me and walked me through what to look for and how to support him along the path. And then, crafty wise woman that she is, she asked how I was doing and if she could have one of the bereavement counselors call me. Blindsided me with that one. She was wise to notice that I would call for help for my son, but probably in a million years would not have called for help for myself. So someone who can help will call me instead, and I am grateful.

The last woman who showed up today was my dear friend Janet. She listened to my story, entertained me with hers, and then, in a brilliant move, quietly and kindly reflected to me a blind spot in my process. Her words touched my bones and helped me see things that were painful but right on the money in terms of what I was feeling but not speaking. She ever-so-gently reflected to me how it must be difficult to keep up with a happy, seemingly non-grieving, child in the midst of my own grief. She wondered if I felt anger towards him that he was able to be so happy. Turns out I am angry. And challenged with how to meet his needs and ways of grieving as well as my own. I don't know how she was able to point that out to me, knowing it was at the risk of me flying completely off the handle. Yet she was able to expose my anger without provoking it. Someone who can do that is truly wise, and I am grateful.

Most importantly, I am aware that I am a reflection of all these wise women. Kind, compassionate, wise, and warm. I can be this for myself and for others, and I can receive from this circle of women. I'm grateful for this advice from my beloved, and I will stand in this circle of wisdom.

Thursday, June 14th

One of the most miraculous things for me right now is what happens to my heart when I see something precious. It must be that I'm so aware of the rawness and the pain that preciousness seems all the more poignant. I was mired in that rawness and pain when I took Lucas out to a local berry barn to pick berries today. It was a struggle to get out of the house. My energy was low, and just the thought of packing up and meeting friends and their children for the afternoon wore me out. But when we arrived, it felt good to be outside and doing something other than just getting through the day at the house.

I was tired though, worn out in a deep-in-the-bones kind of way that made even enjoyable things exhausting. I contemplated this level of fatigue while the kids snacked on fresh raspberries and blueberries. Before long, I was ready to transition back to the emotional safety of home, where I could be sad and not feel like everyone was holding me delicately, as if they thought that at any moment I might break. Feeling so much sadness and yet not being comfortable enough with the setting to talk about it with anyone had sapped me energetically.

And then a miracle happened. A friend showed up with her three-month-old baby. The moment I saw her baby, I absolutely melted—my heart lifted, the fog cleared. Holding that baby and having her sweet, chubby hand grasp my thumb enlivened me and made everything better for a moment. Her leaning toward life and the fresh newness of what it means to be so innocent and open provided the relief I needed to focus on something else, something new, fresh, and completely distracting. Her tiny hand and the wonder of her peaceful face invited me back into the breath of new life and lifted me from the fog of fatigue.

Later that afternoon, my friend Annie brought her puppy over to play with Alta in the backyard. I was tired again when they arrived, but I knew the kids and the dogs needed to play. Then there it was once more, in the exuberant playfulness of her puppy, the movement into bright aliveness that pulled me into a world still moving and growing with each moment.

For the gifts of new life, for puppies and babies, I am grateful.

Friday, June 15th

I had only been up an hour and already there was a long list of things to be grateful for this morning. I was getting ready to leave for a school weekend in California, on my way to a classroom full of people who love me, which on its own is enough for gratitude. And yet in those early morning hours, gratitude for so much more flowed freely.

I am grateful for my sweet little boy who woke up when he heard me get up at four this morning, and who then so gently cozied in and fell back to sleep.

I am grateful for my mom, who is his North Star, and will keep him, along with the house and the dog, happy and running for the weekend.

I am grateful for the warm cup of tea I had time enough to make, but not enough to drink, so it sat precariously on the dash of the car all the way to the airport.

As I drove this morning, I had that amazing sensation of being up early before the rest of the world is awake— the highway empty, moon setting as the sun warms the sky from indigo to blue. It was as if just by being up I had done something noteworthy.

On this morning I am so grateful, and I also desperately miss my loving Michael. I'm on a trip, a school weekend, we had planned to do together. His absence in the car was palpable. But I found music to remind me of his graceful presence and I let myself cry as I drove. As I cried, I had a stunning realization that everything I miss about him is something I am grateful for. Like whenever

I had to get up early and catch a morning flight, he would get up with me to make sure my morning went smoothly and to say goodbye. And the way he knew how to make tea for me perfectly, with just the right amount of honey and a splash of milk. He knew me and was so present for me in his love. It is all those things I miss that now remind me of how grateful I am for having had him in my life.

I see how my gratitude is a reflection of my love for him. And as I go forward, it can be my intention to see the journey of missing him as an exploration of all the things I was grateful for in our love together. My guess is that my heart will become lighter as the list grows longer.

Sunday, June 17th

A rush of gratitude flooded through me as the wheels of the plane safely hit the tarmac this evening. There's something about a massive, metal, pseudo-bird in the sky landing on pavement at high speed that never seems right to me. I'm always grateful to be once again safely on the ground. Tonight there was something more though, because when I left on Friday morning, I promised Lucas I would come back safely. As we landed, I realized how much fear I had been holding around me not coming back safely and not being there for him.

I was worried about leaving so soon anyway. It's only been three weeks, but I needed to go to school down in California to finish a certificate for my master's degree in Spiritual Psychology. I knew the class would be self-honoring, healing, and an act of courage and completion to go to, but I also knew that leaving for three days so soon after Michael's death would be a lot to ask of Lucas.

When I put him to bed Thursday night, we talked about me being gone. His main concern, which he bluntly volunteered, was that I would die, and he wondered who would take care of him. Thankfully he already had a list of people. He told me that if I died my mom, his "Nana," would take care of him, and if something happened to her then Leit would take care of him, and then he went through a list of about ten more people that would care for him if needed.

I was grateful he knew he would always be taken care of, but what hit me strongly was his thinking I would die next. I wanted him to trust that what happened to Michael wasn't going to happen to me, that I would come home after three short days. I didn't want him to worry about losing me. And so, in a moment of either brilliant parenting or a complete parenting bumble, I told him I would be back, and he didn't have to worry about me dying. I promised him I would come home and that we would play Legos on Monday morning. I even did a pinky swear.

But what I realized when I landed tonight is I can't promise him anything. The truth is, we just don't know what's going to happen each day we wake up. I'm not going to saddle him right now with the unpleasant facts of impermanence, but I do realize all I can do is set the intention to be there for him, to take care of myself, to trust that planes will land, and that natural disasters will give us a wide berth. The truth is, I don't know. I also am aware that at any time something new and miraculous could happen. I am just as likely to have a miracle happen as an unthinkable disaster.

Now that I'm safely home and the weekend is over, I'm grateful that I ventured out into the world despite my fear. I'm grateful I felt held in that act of courage, and that I came back in one piece with my heart opened a little more and my confidence buoyed. I can be in the world and not feel like it's going to fall apart around me.

And tonight I careen into my own unsteady landing here at our house. I walk back into all the memories at home and realize I have as much trepidation about my wheels hitting the ground here as I did out on the runway. I want to wake up tomorrow and be able to land softly. I want to trust that I can be as open and loving with myself here at home as I was a thousand miles away.

As I drove down our street toward home, I was aware of a heaviness with the house that felt so big and empty now. I realized how a part of me expected Michael to be home when I got there. I felt myself rock off-balance, just like a plane occasionally bounces on landing and all the passengers gasp.

I wanted to run from the imbalance and from being pulled from my small, newfound confidence into complete breakdown. I had a flash of just packing up the car tonight. I wanted to pick Lucas up out of his bed in the wee hours, still half asleep, and head out on a road trip just to be free of everything familiar that reminds me of Michael. And then, as I pulled in the driveway and saw my dear Alta looking at me by the door, excitedly waiting for me to come home, it all balanced out. I have come home. I am safe here for now with no need to run, and it is my intention to be present tomorrow to that amazing little boy that I crossed pinky fingers with on Friday. I'm home, sweet boy, I'm home.

Wednesday, June 20th

I'm grateful for the smiles I've had in the last few days, doing things that used to get under Michael's skin. The funny thing is, I almost feel him next to me, enjoying how much delight I get out of doing them because I know they won't bother him anymore. We didn't have many habits that got to each other, and the ones we did became constant jokes, as if it was a small way to love the other person by giving in to their idiosyncrasy because it made them so happy.

One thing I noticed last night was the liberation of not having to make the bed at night if I hadn't made it in the morning. It has, in fact, been several nights in a row that I've gone to bed and just flung myself exhausted into a jumble of covers, falling asleep without even thinking of making the bed. That would have driven Michael absolutely insane. He loved straight sheets, un-tucked at the bottom, and pulled right up to the top of the bed. I could care less as long as I have something warm over me. As a result, we had a funny banter, where I would get into bed and be comfortably reading in our "good enough" made bed, and he would come in and need to not only straighten it all out, but lift the covers up and shake them out to be just perfect. It frankly was excruciating to me. Maybe more so after I became a mom, because it would often be the first time I'd had peace in hours, and then I had to endure his active bed making before I could settle in again. But I endured because I loved him.

He loved my patience, and we would co-dependently go to sleep in an odd form of resistance and complete surrender in that small act.

I also notice the subtle liberation of using a dishcloth to wipe the counters in the kitchen. Funny, I know. He was a sponge guy and I am a dishcloth gal. For some reason, he thought dishcloths were germy and I was convinced, especially after microbiology in nursing school, that sponges were the keeper of all things transmissible. I gave in because it really creeped him out to use a dishcloth. I would use a sponge, but I constantly replaced them with new ones, figuring he never had to know sponges were just as gross as dishcloths.

In a similar kitchen-act of grace, he was patient with me leaving cupboards open until I finally broke the habit. Before we got married, he confessed to a friend of mine there was truly only one thing about me he could hardly bear. The confession of this "one thing" was disclosed at my bachelorette party. I felt too old for the standard evening out on the town for a bride-to-be, so my best girlfriends and I gathered for a low-key house party. The food was decadent, cocktails flowed, and I felt cherished. There was some good-natured teasing of me for having taken so long to marry, but everyone was truly celebrating my happiness at being blissfully in love.

When the party games started, I acquiesced even though I had hoped to bypass the traditional ritual of embarrassing the bride-to-be. Most of the games were silly, but the one that revealed my habit was a game where my friend Molly had asked Michael a list of questions, the object being to see if I could guess how he answered. My heart clutched a bit at wondering if something a little too personal might be revealed. Fearfully, I waited for her to expose the truth about my habits in front of all my women friends. I was assuming he'd said something about a seismic flaw in my basic humanness or that I was terrible in bed. But all he told her was that I constantly left drawers and cupboards open in the kitchen. Everyone at the party groaned at such a trivial discovery, but Molly swore that Michael could literally not come up with anything else that bothered him.

It was a tiny habit, and even though I was relieved it was nothing larger, I was sure it was completely untrue. I slipped into self-denial until he walked in the kitchen one day, and I unconsciously had nearly every drawer and cupboard open while I was cooking. He stood there with a slightly amused look on his face that showed how much he adored me until I noticed how obviously right he was about my habit. I was more conscious of it after that, and as I sit in my kitchen this morning, drinking tea and writing, I look around and every drawer and cupboard is shut, as if I'm waiting for him to walk in. He made me a better person, tidy kitchen and all.

In the clothing department, he loved for me to wear color. He didn't buy in to the "black makes me look thin" gig and would pick out colorful things for me. In a magical way, he did it again this last weekend while I was in California for school. Whether it really was him, or a deep memory of how I loved to see him happy when I bought something colorful, his presence was with me, and it caused me to buy something completely out of character.

When I arrived in Los Angeles two dear friends scooped me up from the airport and took me to breakfast. One of them needed to exchange something at REI. When we got to the store, all shiny with the lure of adventure and smell of new gear, I wandered around, not intending to buy anything. By chance, I caught my reflection in the mirror and noticed I was wearing almost all black. My mind flashed to the suitcase I had packed, and I realized everything I brought was black. While it seemed appropriate for the first weekend back to class after Michael's death, it was also kind of sad. Then I noticed, right in front of me, a pink, zip-up, sweater hoodie. It was the exact one Michael had picked out for me in REI just a few months ago. When I tried it on we saw it had a stain on it, and though he scoured the store for the same size, it was the only one. He even offered to get the stain out at home. We didn't buy it then, but here it was now, begging me from its display hangar to buy it and ditch the black. Michael's presence was there with me too, coaxing me not to wear black, encouraging me to live and smile and put a little color on for crying out loud. I bought it and wore it that night, and every time I looked at that hoodie I felt him let me know it was okay to enjoy life in living color, even with him gone.

So I wore my pink hoodie sweater and went out to Mexican food twice on Saturday and the Indian buffet on Sunday. He didn't like Indian food and only enjoyed Mexican food we made at home or at an authentic restaurant.

It wasn't that I felt stilted by not going out to Indian or Mexican food with Michael. There were many other foods we both enjoyed, like sushi or Thai. There was no reason for us not to both love what we were eating. We put our taste buds on hold for the other person, because seeing him uncomfortable was never worth the good taste of the food. Like the way he rarely ate shellfish because I was allergic to it. He could have prepared it separately and tossed it on top of pasta, but he only made it when I was out of town, or he would order it when we went out to dinner. One time each year in Alaska, he and my mom would have a big crab feast when I was out on a hike or at dinner with friends. He loved shellfish and didn't deny himself, but when we cooked together he genuinely wanted to enjoy the same thing. He gave up shellfish and I gave up Indian food and we still lived a full culinary life.

I don't know if there are shellfish in heaven, just as I don't know where he really is, or if we have souls or what they do when we leave this earthly plane. But I hope he's eating shellfish every day and enjoying every bite.

I sense him around me every once in a while, and I can't help but feel there really is more, that my faith in something larger and full of light is real. I am touched by a sense of him every once in a while, and the joy I experience at that moment is deeper than anything I know here on earth. It comes unbidden, like a light breeze upon my face. I sense it as a touch of encouragement, a message to look up, to not only remember the joy, but to understand there is a deeper joy and love than I have ever known. From the other side, he can let me experience this love and joy in a way I never could have with him here. What a gift.

It is a gift much bigger than enjoying Indian food, sponges, colorful clothes, or jumbled covers. A gift of acknowledging my humanness and loving it unconditionally from the other side that lets me know to drop the conditions, the likes and dislikes, and enjoy life in a way that is really about love in the moment. He did that for me here on earth, and I for him. And now, even in my unknowing of where he is or whether what I feel is a memory or a visitation, I trust that the love endures either within me or from some angelic realm, and the way to honor that love is to live. To live in color.

Friday, June 22nd

I'm grateful to be comfortable enough with my vulnerability to admit that I am struggling to find gratitude today. I am slogging through. I don't think it looks like it on the outside, but on the inside I am just getting by. I am admitting that I am keeping busy to avoid the emptiness I feel inside.

I listened to a TED talk last night by a woman named Brené Brown who talked about wholeheartedness. I did this instead of writing, because it all felt so hollow and disheartening. And lo and behold, she talked about wholeheartedness. Which led to her talking about vulnerability and her research showing that people who are connected, who live wholehearted lives, know they are worthy and thus are not as afraid to show their vulnerability. I think that's what she said. But I suppose it doesn't matter, because it's what I heard, and it helped me to go to sleep. Tonight, it is helping me to write once again and to admit that I feel vulnerable.

I feel vulnerable.

I feel like I should be writing to keep the thread intact between grief and gratitude, and instead I am not writing because I'm not feeling any gratitude. I get glimpses but not great bucketsful. How could I? How could I not? My whole experience is a jumble of waves of emotion followed by profound inspiration followed by a mad scrambling busyness carried out in order to not fall into the next giant wave of grief. I am remarkably vulnerable in this mess of emotion, and yet stripped so raw that I can't help but also feel the core of my worthiness. I'm aware that underneath it all there is a place that knows I'll stay connected to it. I know I will find my way back to the love that surrounds me even though Michael has died. The willingness to admit my emotions are carrying me away gives me the distance to understand there is something underneath the emotions I will connect to once again.

And there it is. The gratitude is coming in again, this time on a memory of connection. I'm remembering the steady presence of friends who keep me connected even when I forget to reach out in the midst of busyness or sadness.

Today this connection came in the form of June Bug, my friend Annie's new puppy, who came over again today for a rousing romp in the yard with Alta. Her bouncing puppy persona pulled me out of my sadness and into life again. Annie must have known I needed her connection today, and she was right there, carrying an armful of pure joy.

This brings in the memory of another sweet animal story I'm grateful for, which came in the form of a movie. I cued up a movie tonight, because I frankly didn't have the energy to parent my way through a game night. I needed a movie night, to snuggle on the couch with my little one. We watched *Big Miracle*, about a whale rescue in arctic Alaska. It's the story of how a diverse community with vast differences came together in a vulnerable way in order to save three whales trapped in ice. I think that's what it was about. But what matters in this moment is that was what it was about for me—vulnerability and keeping on despite impossible odds and the knowledge that not all the whales would be saved. In the end, the surviving whales found a path back to freedom aided by an unlikely community of people. They survived by following a path to the sea carved by human hands, and they made it one breath at a time.

I too will survive one breath at a time. But I need help. And help requires vulnerability to ensure that I don't have to take all those breaths alone.

Monday, June 25th

It's late again tonight. The clock is nudging against eleven, and I know that sitting up writing isn't doing my early mornings any favors. It takes me a long time to settle down in the evening. My mind is so wound up from decisions and paperwork and scheduling and going around in circles that I have a hard time getting to sleep. I think it's the going in circles part that's the main problem, and it seems to be getting worse. I'd like to say that things are better, and in some small ways they are. I feel more functional in the world. But underneath, there is this emptiness and general anxiety that keeps me, for lack of a better definition, going in circles. Nothing makes sense—nothing except the moment right in front of my nose. I read in the grief books that cognitive functioning decreases during grief. It does.

And so, without the capacity to recall anything grand, tonight I'll write about the things I found right in front of my nose to be grateful for, which mostly included the act of receiving.

Receiving hasn't been one of my strongest talents up until now. I've always been in the "I'm good, doing okay" kind of category when it came to accepting help. The skill of gracefully receiving from others usually required dire circumstances on my part. I suppose it might be the blood of generations of strong English and Scottish women coursing through my veins in stoic resistance to needing assistance in any way. I'm learning though, that

I need to receive, and I've found, particularly in the last few months, that there is actually a vast amount of vulnerability associated with receiving. Being as vulnerable as I am, I'm getting pretty good at receiving.

It all started this morning with a letter from my master's program I'm trying to finish, and reading the ways in which they're supporting me in finishing all the backlogged homework. I already knew the plan, but the graceful and welcoming way in which the letter was written, instead of in cold academic-speak, opened my heart to see that I really could receive the gift of a little extra time. Just as I was in the midst of crying after reading that letter, a friend of ours called with an offer of assisting me free of charge with a plan to get through varied life details over this next year. She's a professional life coach who specializes in working with women after the loss of a spouse. I knew she could create space for me to process decisions about when to sell the house, how to finish my degree, which direction to move forward professionally, what steps to take with our finances, and how to eventually find a way to tend to all the paperwork that has been piling up these last few months. I was overwhelmed by the magnitude of this offer, considering how much I know she is paid to help other people get through the same details. The offer wasn't up for price negotiation; it was a "take it for free or leave it" situation. And so I said yes. And then I cried some more.

Since I was already having a crying kind of day, I cried my way through the massage that my massage therapist friend gave me. I could have scheduled my own massage, but my weary body just hadn't made the call, and here was one completely planned for me. I sunk in and let my bones be cradled. The thing that was so clear when we said goodbye, was I saw in her eyes how me receiving that massage was a gift to her. I know how fulfilling giving can be, and I'm just now seeing the beautiful gift I open up for myself and for others as I learn to receive in my time of grief.

I opened myself up to a receiving kind of day and it snowballed.

I went to the vet to pick up dog food and one of the vet techs who both my dog and I adore came over to say hello. After one look at me, she offered to meet me for a walk tomorrow on my side of town. She lives far away, so I started to say I could meet her halfway or come over to her side of town, but she stopped me mid-sentence and gave me that "please just let me make this easy for you" kind of look. So I said yes, and then I cried some more.

As I was leaving the vet, I fumbled with picking up the bags of dog food and the receptionist came out from behind the counter and asked if I needed help out to my car. I said yes. The funny thing is, all this receiving seems very removed from any "accept so I can pay it forward" kind of philosophy I've held before. I am accepting and receiving knowing that the circle will come around fully in many small ways as my life plays out over the years to come. The giving and the receiving all feel the same, and the gratitude is spilling over. For now it is spilling over in the form of tears, but I can already feel those tears taking shape and manifesting something new in the world to give.

Tuesday, June 26th

Gratitude and grief are such an unlikely pairing, and yet I'm starting to see at a much deeper level how the two go together. How else could I feel so openly grateful for the support I'm receiving than by also feeling the depths of how hard it is to be facing all this without the love of my life? I'm angry that he's gone, and yet accepting that he's gone. Dichotomous emotions simultaneously inhabit this body of mine.

I walked with a friend today and talked about gratitude for all the support that surrounds me, and she hit it on the head when she said that gratitude within any situation creates elevation. Perhaps that's why it's so important for me to find gratitude each day, because it somehow elevates me. Is it possible to feel grateful simply for gratitude tonight? There needs to be something else besides a general overarching theme, so I'll get specific.

I'm grateful that tonight I had the energy to floss my teeth for the first time in perhaps two months. I'm grateful that I have a house sitter for our dog when we leave to have Michael's memorial service in Alaska next month. I'm grateful for the fresh, cool water that comes straight out of the tap here in our lush northwest environment. I'm grateful that my sister and her boys are safe despite the fires raging in Colorado.

Which brings me out of my gratitude list and into my senses. This fire challenges my belief that I am the only one going through the experience of grief and loss.

There are people very specifically in Colorado today who have also fallen into that great abyss.

My sister sent me a photo of the hills on fire just outside Colorado Springs, where her partner was called out on the fire fighting team to get the fire under control. The whole state seems to be on fire, and the temperature is pushing one hundred degrees each day with no rain in sight. Entire neighborhoods are burning, and I see the reality of life and death in a world where there is clear evidence I am not alone in any of this grief.

People die each day and leave spouses, children, and families. People die of cancer, soldiers die in war, cars crash, and wildfires burn. There is no escape, and yet this is not where our minds want to go when we think about our lives each day. The normal routines and satisfactions are not necessarily full of thoughts of grief and potential trauma, but neither are they full of gratitude. Which brings me full circle to understanding how grief and gratitude go together. How rarely do we acknowledge how good we've got it just because we can get up and breathe each day?

I feel for every family tonight who is being evacuated because of a forest fire, and I feel for every widow tonight who is going to bed alone without their loved one. Remarkably, I am grateful this knowledge of grief is leading me toward more grace and gratitude in the awareness of how precious everything is in this world. I pray our moments be filled with this awareness as the sun sets on sweet children sleeping in warms beds and rises to see us greeting it with the expectation of something good happening this new day. I pray we might know the blessing it is to simply be alive and not alone in this human experience.

Wednesday, June 27th

It's been one month now since Michael died, and I am aware how the world I see these days might have been one only of darkness and shadows. Yet through gratitude and grace, what I also see is a world that is kind, gentle, supportive, and uplifting. There are plenty of challenges in my days, and there are times when I find myself frustrated with the busy, harsh energy of the world, and I wish things could be softer. I wish we could all treat one another as if a tragedy has just happened in our lives. I wish we could treat one another with openness, softness, and a place of comfort where a tender soul can rest. And yet, as I walk through the world looking for gratitude each day and reflect on it each night, I realize that what I am seeing are the graceful and gracious parts of life. My focus is on the beautiful, and it is becoming what I see despite the grief.

This focus on gratitude and the world I am seeing through those eyes brought me to a memory of Michael in the week or two before he died. He would ask that he not be left alone upstairs and wanted someone near even when he was sleeping. He explained to me how hard it was to wake up alone and away from the world. Mostly he was unable to get out of bed. So when he woke and heard any of us downstairs, he had a longing to be part of things that at times was unbearable. We made a commitment to always have one of us sit with him and be there for him when he woke. He knew he would eventually need to take his final journey alone, but he didn't have to be alone quite yet. The world still called to him, and I think in the end, when for so many days he struggled to live despite the suffering he was enduring, he wanted to be in the world simply for how much he loved his life. He loved this world of ours that calls us to be part of it; that is made for us to be completely drawn into while we are incarnate on this planet.

I've spent a lot of my life feeling as if I wanted to be separate from the world; that the world itself was some sort of lure into a depth of humanness that felt a little too messy for me. In many ways, I avoided being too engaged or committed, and until I met Michael I don't think I was fully embodied. But he loved life so much, and got such pleasure in the simple joys of what makes us human, fully embracing his human self. I learned more about delicious food and wine, great poetry, beautiful music, and pure sensuality in my eight years with him than I had in the thirty-six prior. As I said to a friend the other day, "Michael was worth risking full embodiment." I was able to open to my entire range of humanness to be fully with him in the world. He made me want to live, without worrying about high cholesterol or whether I was staying up too late. He expanded my horizon of what it meant to live, and for this I am eternally grateful.

I don't know what it will be like when I am close to dying. Yet Michael's experience has given me a taste of what it feels like to yearn to be a part of life that has become elusive. So I try each day in my yoga practice to take savasana to heart; to really embrace this final position known as "corpse pose" as the practice, each and every day, of letting go. When I lie in savasana, completely relaxed, my body and mind sinking into the floor and releasing attachments, I feel this dichotomy: the incredible freedom in letting go matched with a greater pull toward the life that calls to me from the edges of my pose. I hear the birds outside reminding me of the splendor of morning and the rumblings of the world beyond my windows beginning to embrace the day. Life calls to me, reminding me to embrace it, to go and see the world with gratitude for all the gifts awaiting me when I open my door.

Thursday, June 28th

I found out yesterday how to be grateful for my shoes. It all started innocently enough, as I graciously waited in the post office for the clerk to discover why the one piece of mail that I have sent certified in my entire life was the one piece of mail that precisely did not make it to its destination. I wasn't happy, but I was resigned to the growing reality that two certified death certificates plus every piece of identifying information for Michael and I, along with the life insurance forms, were lost somewhere in the ether between Portland, Oregon and Omaha, Nebraska. I stood patiently, waiting to learn the fate of the certified package, holding a new set of forms to mail off again, when right next to me came a bubbling bride-to-be. Piles and piles of wedding invitations fell out of her giddy hands and tumbled onto the counter.

What bizarre twist of fate would have me standing with a handful of death certificates and insurance forms for my departed beloved and her there just beginning the journey of love? I noticed the irony of how I too thought my love would last forever when I stamped those invitations to our magical wedding. The blissful edges of that memory brushed against me then in a flash the moment was gone. I quickly realized I was going to lose it if I didn't do something fast.

I needed a focus point to keep me steady, so I suddenly became grateful for my shoes. My toes pressed into their soles and my heels grounded into their fit. I felt every inch of my shoes and said a little prayer of gratitude for them holding me up as I found my breath and steadied myself on the counter. The clerk came back a moment later, reassuring me that the package would be found, and took the time to walk me through mailing the new one. When I turned to leave, the bride was gone, off to pick out napkins or a cake I'm sure, and I walked back to the car feeling grateful for my shoes and for making it through yet another blindside wave of grief.

I loved our wedding and the piles of invitations. But that event is so surreal now, as if because he's gone it never happened. I couldn't relate to that bride-to-be at all. I just felt jaded and sad.

It hurt, and yet I know it won't be like this forever. On the way home, I remembered how Michael made wonderful playlists of music for us every summer, and we would dance in the living room until we had to throw ourselves on the couch in exhaustion. The memories are still there, still beautiful, and still available to remind me how much we loved each other. Yet I still don't want to think of brides or wedding or invitations. I'm grateful to make it through the flood of memories today, but I think I'll hold off on attending any weddings. I don't think I can find a stable enough pair of shoes. Heels just don't quite lend themselves to steadiness in the midst of grief.

Friday, June 30th

I had a good gratitude groove going earlier today. I was so incredibly thankful for our little portable document shredder. I took every single piece of cancer-related paper and shredded it to pieces. It felt so liberating, as if I was shredding the memories of the treatments, the side effects, the worrying, right along with the physical evidence those papers showed of the cancer that was growing inside of him. This time last year, the paperwork was impossible to keep up with, so it ended up piled everywhere in the office. I went through every piece, and unless it had to do with the medical bills—which unbelievably are still coming in—I shredded and dumped it. Done. It felt good but strange, as if the whole last year and a half was just some weird pile of misfiled papers. So much hope lived in those papers, and so much despair, all mixed in as crazy documentation of the journey we had with cancer.

When I finished shredding, it was time to head over to dinner at a friend's house. From the high feelings of completion that shredding afforded me, I walked into a full-on grief trigger. I'd been looking forward to spending time with our friends, but as soon as I walked in the door I realized how odd it was to not have Michael there. I was completely blindsided, broadsided, leveled.

And never missed a beat.

Smiled, had a glass of wine, got settled into conversations, and tried my best to have a nice evening, while the palpability of his absence sat heavy in the room. They were two of our best friends as a couple: fabulous cooks, great conversationalists, and we had nice evenings with the kids entertaining themselves while we adults enjoyed time talking around the table. But tonight I was there as a single—made even more obvious by them having invited another couple who are dear friends of ours—and it felt so odd without Michael.

I realized how we all loved him, and even though we all missed him, we didn't talk about him, except on the edges of conversation. I didn't want to bring him up, because I knew I would start sobbing, and I suppose they didn't bring him up for the very same reason. I went to the bathroom near the end of dinner and let myself cry a bit. Then on the way home, in the car's darkness, I let the tears roll down my face, no longer able to hold them back.

I miss him. I miss him terribly, and I see how hard it is to go on doing things without him that we always enjoyed together. Our friends are lovely, and they will be there for me. And I'm grateful. And it was hard.

This was another first time doing something that hopefully makes the second time easier or more graceful, or maybe not. Maybe I can be more authentic next time and express my grief more openly, or maybe I'll not talk about it again. I can't guess what this journey is going to be like, any more than I could have guessed how good it would feel to shred all those papers today. One step at a time, one memory at a time, finding my way into the future, trusting that I will be graceful and authentic some day, but for now just grateful to be present to the process.

July

"*Grief and gratitude are kindred souls, each pointing to the beauty of what is transient and given to us by grace.*"

– Patricia Carlson

Sunday, July 1st

Today, I'm grateful for spaciousness. I created a little spaciousness with all that paper shredding yesterday, but what I really need is some wide, open space in which to breathe. I feel claustrophobic; whether with clutter, or being in a loud place, or being in a crowd. I need more room. I know it's grief keeping me tender around the edges, and giving it space helps me to not bump up against myself or anyone else.

When I walk these days, I give myself space by going to the twenty-acre park a few miles from our house, even though it's a bit of a drive. I'm free there and can shed my tears without running into someone every five minutes. I used to walk in our neighborhood, or in our little village town center within the bigger confines of the city, but it's too busy now for me. I want the perimeter of green openness the park has to offer. I can't take the loudness of cars or multiple people passing by. I'm sensitive these days, and it's not just my small-town Alaskan roots.

My sensitivity is such that I'm now careful about what I get myself into, even while trying to enjoy summer with Lucas off of school. So when my friend asked me to go swimming with the kids today, I hesitated because I knew it would be crowded at the indoor pool. But Lucas loves to swim, and we needed to get out of the house, so I agreed. When we got to the pool, it was at capacity. We had to put our name on a waiting list for a spot to open up and even that small task felt exhausting. I started to panic at the thought of a pool full of people, of being in a loud, wet cacophony. I didn't think I could handle it. I had the irrational feeling I needed to run away.

I mentioned the outdoor pool to my friend, which I didn't think she would go for since it was raining. But she was also overwhelmed at the thought of keeping track of kids in a maxed-out pool, so we headed off for an outdoor swim when it was sixty degrees and raining. And it turned out to be heaven. We were the only ones in the entire pool, and the water was blissfully warm in comparison to the chill of the afternoon. We only lasted an hour, but a graceful spaciousness opened up for me, so I actually enjoyed swimming with my boy and our friends.

I'm grateful for the space and open air, and mostly I'm grateful to those two hundred people who filled up the other pool and left a grieving mom with a midday miracle.

Monday, July 2nd

Today, I tasted the first fresh blueberries of summer and realized that a year ago, Michael and I were picking blueberries in our own yard. This year our poor yard is barely hanging on; it takes care of itself with an occasional mow and the grace of intermittent rain.

I know the sweetness of summer is bursting from these first few berries of the season, but I can barely taste anything these days.

I'm numb. Eating is an effort. I want my life back.

I'm also aware that one day I will have to sell the house. I will sell the house and with it all of our berry bushes. I wonder about the house and life to come. Will there be blueberries in our yard? Will I someday taste them with sweetness instead of sadness?

Tuesday, July 3rd

Tonight, I'm grateful for the little boy giggles that infuse my days with love and laughter. As we left the grocery store tonight, we were chewing the gum we'd bought, and Lucas wanted me to teach him how to blow a bubble. Having never actually explained how to blow a bubble, I found myself floundering as I tried to talk and navigate the mouth movements it took to make a single bubble. He tried his best to follow along, but every time he just made a funny *Phlepp!* sound, and he laughed hysterically.

By the time we got to the car, he was laughing so hard he could barely stand up and his giggling had me in stiches as I loaded the groceries. For a moment I saw us as the rest of the world must have seen us—a mother and son laughing in the parking lot. I saw us as happy. All because of bubble gum. I didn't have to let myself be happy, or think about being happy, or try to be happy. I just laughed at my beautiful boy trying to blow bubbles and was simply happy.

I'm aware of some of the judgments I have around being happy. I judge myself for not being solemn enough, because I believe being happy is betraying the grief I feel so deeply. I also fear what will people think if they see me happy. Perhaps they'll wonder if I shouldn't be home crying instead. On a more rational level, I know that my feelings or expressions of happiness and joy have nothing to do with the grieving process. I want to remember that it is not only acceptable, but actually incredibly supportive, to be in situations where I can feel happiness. I'm aware of how my ability to feel happiness relates to the amount of authentic emotion I'm able to express all the way around.

I've been crying a lot the last couple of days, overwhelmed with the weight of a future so uncertain. But I believe letting the anguish come through is also what has created space for the joy to come through. I'm not as numb anymore, as the anesthetic of shock wears off. I'm living in the world, going to the grocery store, buying gum, blowing bubbles, and laughing.

Tomorrow, we're going to a friend's vacation house for a few days. I'm aware that among the opportunities for laughter, there will quite possibly be occasions of loneliness and grief in the midst of this time with other families. I'm willing to feel it all. I want to engage both the grief and the joy because I don't want to miss a moment of laughter with my bright boy. I open myself to more happiness—and I know now to be sure and take an extra pack of gum.

Wednesday, July 4th

Today was the Fourth of July, and I found myself in anxiety's tight grip like I have never experienced. A friend invited us to spend the weekend in Sunriver, and I accepted, relieved to have somewhere to go, somewhere to be other than home to experience this first holiday without my beloved friend and partner. It seemed doable, realistic, and wise—until I started out on the road. I had packed the car alone, gotten the bags together, and done a sweep through the house. Painful as it was to do all those things by myself, I felt strong and clear, like I could meet the drive with courage even if a few tears leaked through along the way.

We got an hour or so down the road, and I felt confident, but when it came time to get gas, I panicked. I couldn't find a station and had to go several miles off our route. I was driving Michael's car, and when I finally pulled into a station, I realized the gas tank was on the other side. So I had to maneuver around and try again. By the time I fueled up and drove away, I was so riddled with anxiety that I had to pull over and go through my mental inventory of what I needed: child, dog, keys, wallet, phone. An hour later, we stopped to go to the bathroom and again the anxiety edged in. I used my mantra—child, dog, keys, wallet, phone—as if I might somehow forget the dog on the side of the road or leave my child playing in a park somewhere and not remember until fifty miles later. Unrealistic, irrational, unstable, one might say.

I made it though, down to the vacation house, my jangled nerves humming in the background and the anxiety relatively at bay. My mantra had kept me safe, trusting that all I needed were those important items. But underneath, I was concerned about this unexpected anxiety manifesting in my life.

Enter my friend Hillary, our weekend host, who asked me how I was doing. I confessed that even though we'd just arrived, I was already overwhelmed with anxiety about making the drive home alone and returning to an empty house. To me, admitting my anxiety was like sharing a dangerous secret. Yet with one sentence, she erased my fear and welcomed me into a world where anxiety was manageable and fear a trusted friend. Hillary told me she had also experienced anxiety at different times in her life and would be comfortable talking about it with me if I wanted some help.

I've yet to take her up on her offer, because in that one moment she cured me of fearing anxiety simply by admitting it was a normal reaction to a life-changing event. Her candid response created the space for healing, a place where a new emotion I had never tangibly felt before suddenly was simply a place that needed support.

Over this last couple of months, I've learned quite a bit about the nuances of grief and anxiety, and how a world shattered by death compromises one's core fears about comfort, security, and control, allowing anxiety to creep in unexpectedly. My learning came over time, but the key I needed in that moment, that one terribly frightening moment when the world shifted beneath me, was a friend telling me that anxiety is a normal reaction with possibilities for coping. In this way, her story was a gift: one of releasing stigmas and trusting that symptoms are pathways to healing, one that recognizes the universality of the human condition and trusts that we are all, in one way or another, on the path to wholeness.

Saturday, July 7th

A recurring theme at the moment is the dichotomy of feeling so much gratitude and joy in the midst of so much grief and sadness. The last few days of vacationing with friends saved us from the sadness of being alone on the Fourth of July. I cried and laughed more this last weekend than I have in a while. Most days I've been fulfilled with hikes, bike rides, playing in the pool, yoga on the banks of the Deschutes River, and general family fun in the high desert of Oregon. I also had nourishing time in the evenings with women friends, where I felt heard, cherished, and held.

Despite this lovely, full weekend, last night I experienced a flood of sadness when we all talked about leaving. My throat tightened and my heart started to feel intensely heavy. I could barely speak, the thought of going home to an empty house hit me so hard. Then, because it was just too much to hold back, I went ahead and let myself cry, sharing the pain as easily as I had shared the laughter a few moments before.

I ride up and down the rollercoaster of so many emotions that today I wasn't terribly surprised when I found myself crying not out of fear or sadness, but out of gratitude for the kindness of our children. We were all headed out for a bike ride and one of the kids in the group got shy and embarrassed, thinking she wasn't as strong a rider as the rest of the kids. She hugged her mom while three other children waited patiently for her to gather

her courage. Then Lucas said, "I believe in you!" and the other kids chimed in.

She got up and going on her bike again and when she got shaky a short while later, they all stopped and waited for her without any complaint or urgency, even though I could sense them feeling antsy to get going to the park. Lucas offered his bike up, since it was a little smaller than hers. This time when she got going, they all cheered her on, "Go! You did it! Yahoo!" I got all teary, I was so touched by the gentle kindness they shared. Essentially, it gave me hope the world could hold me gently too right now. That I have supporters encouraging me with "You can do it! I believe in you!" as I get up my courage to begin once again.

Later in the day, Lucas and I began our drive home. Because I was terrified of arriving early to an empty house with hours stretching before bedtime, I offered up a trip to Lava Lands National Park. Lucas jumped on the adventure bandwagon.

It was all a great idea until we pulled into Lava Land's parking lot. The temperature had reached 95 degrees, and I knew we would need to take Alta with us rather than leave her in the car. We got up to the head of the interpretive trail and were headed out to explore when we realized we would roast on this field of black lava in the blistering sun. I worried about Alta's paws burning on the hot path and we, of course, didn't have any water with us. The walk in this heat would have been a stretch on any day, but on this day I knew it was too much to even try.

We abandoned the fiery walk and headed to the visitor center, where I found myself with a disappointed child, a dog I couldn't leave outside, and no husband to help out. My edges were fraying until I realized my life from here on out depended on learning to navigate the world of solo parenting. So, reassured by the ranger that there was no back door from which he could disappear, I let Lucas go into the visitor center to investigate things on his own with his promise to keep checking back in. Once again he pushed my gratitude button by sticking his little face out the door every five minutes and then running back in to check out some more volcanic fun facts. He got that we were in this together and that I needed his cooperation to make this little extravaganza to Lava Land work out.

I think by the end of the trip we were both grateful and reassured that we can go on adventures on our own and manage the dog, the car, the packing, the directions, and the mandatory soft serve ice cream stops. I've no doubt that we have angelic intervention in our favor, but I also am aware that seeing the world through the eyes of gratitude is like having my own little posse of six-year-olds cheering me on as I find my balance again. "You can do it! I believe in you!"

And for this I am phenomenally grateful.

Sunday, July 8th

Maybe I like to focus on gratitude and grace so I can believe there actually are such moments. The reality is that life now is not always inspiring or uplifting. In fact tonight it was quite ugly. I completely lost my patience with Lucas. It was late and hot and I was tired. He seemed set on pushing me to the limit by not listening and making bath and bedtime impossible and eternal.

I gave the evening all my patience and then I yelled. Not just kind of yelled, but really yelled. And then I cried. Then I apologized and cried some more. And then I went around the corner and sobbed while he sat there in the bathtub, stunned to silence. It really scared him; the crying and the yelling, and I felt absolutely terrible. I was angry. At him a little, in a normal parent-out-of-patience kind of way, but deeper than that I was angry with Michael for not being here.

I'm angry, and I don't like having to do it alone every night. I'm lost a lot of the time when I'm alone and worn thin and trying to get through the routine so I can have a few minutes to myself. I don't like "getting through" to describe any of my parenting, but there are times when it does, and tonight was one of those times.

I don't like yelling, and yet I'm grateful for remembering to be gentle with myself. To forgive myself and to ask forgiveness from Lucas when I scare him with my "mommy losing it" routine. And to remind him that my agreement to not yell also goes along with his agreement to cooperate and listen, even just a little. So I have extra melancholy tonight, wondering if I broke his belief in me a bit. I'll try again tomorrow. I made as much peace with it tonight, with him and with myself, as I could. I guess there's some redeeming value in teaching a child that people can lose it and still recover. I also see how much I'm in need of help and support and kindness. I can do this, although I also know that it will take time.

Tuesday, July 10th

I'm grateful today to have slept in until seven, and thereby feel rested and able to greet the ups and downs with a little more grace. Yesterday started at five in the morning, waking to the sound of Alta about to throw up. There's nothing quite like the sound of a dog throwing up, particularly in a carpeted bedroom. I didn't get her outdoors, but I did get her downstairs to the hardwood floor, where the offending stick made its way out after a fitful night in her stomach. After taking care of her, I thought I was home-free to spend a couple of hours in meditation, yoga, and writing. Then, at quarter past five, just as I finished making my tea, Lucas called down to say he was awake . . . sigh.

The day spiraled further toward fatigue when I ran into one of the moms from Lucas's school. She'd just found out about Michael and really felt the need to give condolences right there in the middle of soccer camp drop-off. That exhausting exercise of patiently accepting her condolences in a completely awkward setting was followed by a phone call from a friend who didn't seem to hear me when I said I was struggling and needed to get off the phone. Close on the heels of that call came someone else asking me if I could watch their child that afternoon, and to whom I actually told the truth, saying I was absolutely exhausted and wondering if I could find enough patience for my own child, much less an additional one. And then I cried.

It got better from there, with a soulful walk with my friend Kimberly, an afternoon swim with Lucas in an outdoor pool, and an evening walk in the sunshine. But until this morning, I never quite got over the exhaustion, which is why today was such a better day.

In celebration of a relatively stable day, I actually cooked something. Not a full meal or anything, but we were headed to a barbeque, so I rummaged in the bottom of my fridge crisper and came up with a red onion and some broccoli which I promptly turned into a delicious broccoli slaw with the help of lime, yogurt, and fresh parsley out of the garden. I was amazed with myself! Not only was I about to eat something healthy, but I actually participated in its creation, which is a far cry from anything I've done this last month. Perhaps it's because I had macaroni and cheese for lunch, which is so much the antithesis of Portlandia's green, gluten-free eating fare that it tipped me over the edge in search of something cruciferous. I'm grateful to be eating something green.

While I'm on the topic of food, I also have to express gratitude for my friends up in Alaska who are taking on organizing the food for Michael's memorial service and Celebration of Life there later this month. I was strung out trying to plan things from here, and one evening on the phone a friend said in a most brilliant way, "Can I just take that on for you?" She didn't say, "Let me know if there's anything I can do to help." She actually said she wanted to take care of it so I didn't have to worry about it at all. Hallelujah.

Helping someone in grief can be tricky. What I'm finding is that when people say, "Let me know if there's anything I can do to help," what they might really be saying is "I have no idea how to help you, I'm uncomfortable, and I want to make this better, and I don't know how." Which leaves us both in a place of feeling helpless. I know I should have a list of things I need help with, but it's hard to ask people to do something that you're not sure they want to do.

What I really want is someone to mow the lawn, or clean out the garage, or make me a super healthy, green dinner and just drop it off spontaneously on the very night I'm contemplating whether or not I can get away with a quesadilla for one more meal. In truth, there's not much that can make me feel good. It hurts no matter whether my lawn is mowed or not, but I'm grateful for friends who think of things that might be helpful and jump in and take care of them. We could all use a little more of that, grieving or not grieving, to come home to a surprise that eases the burden.

There's the easing of emotional burdens too, which I observed with amazing gratitude this evening at a gathering. The night went pretty smoothly, and I was with close enough friends that we were able to talk about Michael and have it be comfortable. There was grilling, good conversation, and flag football with kids on one team and parents on the other, until the dusk brought the evening to a close.

There was this moment, right before we all left, where we took pictures, first of the kids, then all of us gals, and then all the adults piled on a bench in the yard. And in one brief moment, I realized the adults had sat as the three couples they were. The pain emerged sharp and new in the recognition of Michael's obvious absence. My friends swooped in without a word between any of us and literally shape-shifted the configuration so it was just a mixture of adults, all sharing an evening. There would have been a hole in the picture if we hadn't moved around, an obvious space next to me where Michael would have been smiling, his cheeks rosy from the games in the yard, and his dimples bright on his face as he reveled in the company of good friends. As it was, there was the joy of friendship and the keen awareness of a moment recovered and shifted into something new—not forgetting the old, but honoring the bond we now share in the loss of a partner and good friend. A few tears followed, but the night was soft on all of us. The evening of activity lulled us off to our cars with kids in tow and toward the comfort of a good night's sleep after an evening well spent. And for this night, I feel deep gratitude.

Thursday, July 19th

This last week has been a blur, trying to get ready for our trip to Alaska. I've been too overwhelmed and exhausted to write at night. There have been all the tangible things to do, getting ready for the two-week trip, but also the emotional preparation as well. Alaska in so many ways feels like going home, and being home without Michael feels so deeply out of alignment.

Both Michael and I grew up in Alaska, but it wasn't until later in life that we met, fell in love, had Lucas, and made our home. The memories are thick here and friendships run deep. Having the memorial service in Portland for Michael felt like something we needed to do, but the one in Juneau will be the one he asked for, where the old friends from childhood, work, and play will all gather. The people who truly knew him will be here.

We planned everything for the Saturday service from afar, and now Lucas and I are finally here, settling into my mom's house. Looking back on the last couple of days of travel, I see both the challenges and the blessings. Tonight I'm grateful to be able to laugh at things that otherwise would make me cry—particularly bringing Michael's ashes back to Alaska. I thought bringing remains to a final resting place would be a solemn event, but several times I caught myself laughing at the awkwardness of having his ashes in my backpack.

At airport security in Portland yesterday, our bags went through the scanner and I cringed when my backpack was stopped mid-screen. The security agent eyed me then looked back at the scanner screen the way they do when they're thinking about pulling your bag out for inspection. Then she just nodded at me in a knowing kind of way, let the bag go through, and we were off. I felt strangely like I was getting away with something; transporting something suspicious. It seems like our culture views death and its accouterments as strange and scary things, as if they should be hidden, secretly tucked away.

This morning in Seattle security, they weren't nearly as inconspicuous. They had no qualms taking a closer look and running several tests on the box of ashes. I felt completely naked standing there trying to keep an eye on Lucas as they took the box out of my backpack, unwrapped it from its beautiful silk cloth, and coarsely dusted it down for several tests. Explosives? Drugs? Seriously? I found myself so incredibly vulnerable that I had to perception-check whether I wanted to make this a complete injustice propelling me into a burst of outrage, or a hilarious anomaly that needed a little humor. I found a sweet spot in between, a small chuckle with a dose of indignation, and then again we were off, with the box in my backpack feeling just a little heavier than before.

I didn't think about the ashes much again until we got off the plane in Juneau and were greeted by several friends, one of whom offered to carry my bags. I said my backpack was heavy, but she insisted, and I passed it reluctantly to her without revealing the contents. I was afraid it would be a little over-the-edge for her. She moaned and groaned all the way to baggage claim about how heavy it was, along with the requisite questions about whether or not I'd brought my rock collection. I didn't say a word, even though several easily inappropriate ways of breaking it to her went through my mind. But the shock factor would have been too high, and dark humor falls flat these days to those who are seeing me for the first time since Michael's death. I'm not sure whether it's me being gentle with them or them being gentle with me. Either way, I let it go, when inside I wanted to either make a joke or burst into tears. I ended up making a small comment to my mom on the side, which made her laugh and eased the tension. I hadn't realized how hard it would be to come home with his ashes on my back and greet everyone who loved him so much.

Now the ashes sit on my bedside table awaiting the service on Saturday. They're comforting here next to me, and yet so completely removed from my awareness of him. It's a strange mix of fascination and reassurance. I don't know how I will feel on Sunday when we go out on the water to scatter them near his favorite island. I don't have any expectation for closure. I want to think that scattering his ashes will ease the feeling that something is incomplete. He was so clear about his wishes for his body after death, and I know I'm attending to the appropriate rituals by scattering his ashes here in the place he knew as home. I know it's something I want to do, need to do, and promised him I would do. I don't want to hang on to them, but is it too soon? Should I wait and come back next year? I can't imagine waiting as much as I can't imagine letting them go.

I'm aware the ashes are simply a symbol of his earthly presence, and yet there's something deeply sacred about them. I can't bear the thought of leaving them here, but neither can I think of carrying them all the way home again. As it stands now, the marine forecast is for three-to-six foot seas on Sunday, so we'll see if Mother Nature has a say. I trust we will find our way, in stormy weather or calm. A storm seems fitting, but at the same time I'm holding out hope that the seas will still and the sun will shine and this leg of the journey will feel more spiritual and less vulnerable than the trip here. I hope for some sense of peace and perhaps some light humor, along with an understanding that this is just one more leg of a much longer journey.

Saturday, July 21st

I am stunned once again by all the love that surrounds us. We had Michael's memorial service and Celebration of Life today. So much love. So many memories of not just who he was to me, but what he meant to other people as well. There was a formal service at the Episcopal Church at Michael's request, out of what I think was respect for my family tradition. Then there was a more informal celebration up at the local ski lodge, which was a fitting tribute to his adventurous spirit. The most beautiful thing about today was that I could rest in the arms of community. The food was a potluck, the flowers hand-picked by friends who had gathered them from the mountain outside the lodge, and the words spoken were straight from the heart of anyone who wanted to speak. He was loved, we are loved, and despite how challenging it has been to take it all in and to have his death seem more real in the face of everyone else's expression of grief, there are moments of support today that I will remember for my entire life.

Tuesday, July 24th

Two days have passed since we scattered Michael's ashes, and I'm just now feeling gratitude around how the day worked out. It helped yesterday to go out on the water again, to fish for halibut and witness whales sounding and spouting, as the seas stayed calm for yet another un-expected day of reprieve from weather moving in.

It hurts still to think of the day when we released his ashes into the water. There is the tightness of tears be-hind my eyes, and a choke in my throat as the grief comes up again for more release, more letting go, more assimi-lation of the reality of what has happened.

I'm tender and tired now. I want to stay inside and sleep rather than go out and be in the beauty of the Alaskan waterways that were our home. There is relief in having completed what we came here to do. The world still beckons, invites me to experience its grandeur, but it competes with the contraction of wanting to experi-ence the more compelling inner landscape of grief and letting go. So I stay somewhere in the middle and rest today before going back out to walk the beach. When I take to the water again, with the hum of the motor be-neath me, and the wind on my face, the lull of the waves against the hull, they will remind me that the deep sea below is still alive and vibrant with life.

It is that lull that reminds me of Sunday. The waves gently nudged the side of the boat and rocked us in our quiet solitude there by the island where the blue-green sea absorbed his ashes and the flowers moved away slowly with the current, one large peony shining in bright pink contrast to the shades of blue, gray, and green that surrounded us.

I felt relief and a deep sadness, as if he had gone away from me in a way that was irretrievable and yet also completely inevitable. I had completed what he asked me to do, released his ashes into the water there on Shaman Island, and there was peace in having fulfilled that final wish for him of a place to rest.

Was it relief for me or for him? I don't know.

I hadn't imagined there would be any attachment to the ashes, and yet the morning we were to release them, I lay in meditation after a yoga class and had a half dream. I felt his spirit pulling me toward the island, out of the clouds, over the water, towards his resting place. When I came out of that space of dreaming and into full waking, a sense of urgency came over me, a need to rush towards completion.

When I got back to my mom's house, there was a message from the friend taking us out on his boat that day to spread the ashes. He was concerned about the weather; there was forecasted to be a small craft advisory later that afternoon. He wanted to leave early, and there's nothing like urgency in a boat captain's voice to create incentive for quick preparation. A few moments later, we were in the car and headed out to the beach by his house. Within an hour we were on the boat and out on the water, headed across the bay while the seas were still calm.

I felt unprepared, rushed, and on a course uncontrollable by me. A course drawn by something much larger than my own need for something sacred, organized, thought-out, and prepared. In the end, no words were clear enough to mark the moment. So we said few and each person took a moment to scatter a handful of ashes into the water before I released the larger amount down into the blue-green depths. Then each threw a flower out into the water in commemoration of our own expression of remembrance.

I remember the silence that then fell, each of us staring at the island with tears flowing. And I remember the blue of the sky, the sun shining through the clouds, and the calm seas, all emerging from within the shadow of a rainy, windy forecast that never transpired.

It was a perfect day, and the water absorbed his ashes in a sweet release that felt light and clear. The water rocked us in the boat; a quiet press of waves that drifted farther and farther from the island.

As we slowly pulled away, my heart ached deeper than it had before, in a clear finality to the day. I realized that without the urgency I may have faltered or stumbled in following through with the release of his ashes. I may have wanted to hold on, but it was the careening motion that propelled me to let go, to free the ashes of his earthly inhabitance and release them into the oneness of the water, to free them from their journey and into the welcoming arms of the sea.

The next day on the water was healing to my tender heart. I saw the island in the distance as we watched humpback whales surfacing and heard seagulls circling above, awaiting their feast of fresh herring. Life was all around us while in the distance the island stood as a symbol of the very preciousness of the aliveness we embody. Today I will go out to the water again, feel the tides pull in and out, sit on the beach and watch the shifts of movement from day to dusk, and remember that life still calls in every wave. I will quietly remember the space between the waves is meant for my own breath, a movement in and out, that symbolizes life and all that awaits me in the coming tide.

Friday, July 27th

I'm grateful today for good weather. I'm usually a "There's no such thing as bad weather, only bad gear" kind of gal, but I have to admit that it being dry and relatively warm these last couple of weeks in Alaska has been a precious gift. Oddly enough, the weather shifted on our way out to the airport for our return home. The rain started to make its way down the channel, and by the time we took off, the valley was completely socked in with clouds, and rain was beating against the windows.

This evening back in Portland, I'm trying to find something to be grateful for, and I found it when I remembered seeing Mt. St. Helens out the airplane window this morning. What a wonder of the natural world. Amazing to see the crater and realize it was over thirty years ago that it erupted. I was awestruck at seeing it up close as we flew over.

I needed a strong memory from today to write about, as coming home has left me sad and overwhelmed. The house feels empty, the days stretch ahead with no end in sight, and I'm on my own with everything, especially parenting. Alta's allergies kicked in while we were gone, and her paws are raw and hurting. I'm overwhelmed by her care, by the house and yard, and by parenting alone once again without the presence of family. I want to remember beautiful things so I don't get caught up in how sad and alone I feel.

So I'm grateful for the wonder of seeing Mt. St Helens up close and personal.

I'm grateful for one last walk in Juneau this morning with my friend Kathy, which felt authentic and connected.

I'm grateful for the woman at the PDX airport who smiled back at me when we walked in to the terminal.

I'm grateful for our friend Nick, who picked us up at the airport with Alta.

I'm grateful for our dog sitter leaving the house so clean.

I'm grateful that the weather has been temperate and my garden is still alive.

I'm grateful there was a frozen pizza in the freezer.

I'm grateful the Olympics are on so the evening didn't seem so long.

I'm grateful for my sweet boy Lucas and his amazing resiliency, courage, and maturity. What a gift he is in my world.

August

"Do we ever really die when we have lived so clearly in one another's hearts?"

Wednesday, August 8th

I've just returned home from California after an intense week attending my final practicum for a master's certificate program in Consciousness, Health, and Healing. This trip and the five days of intensive experiential study were the last things I had to do in order to finish, and at times I desperately wanted to let it all go.

Being away from Lucas and home for so long so soon has been a challenge. But the real challenge has been engaging in the work required of me as a student to explore my own healing. I had originally applied to the program with Michael, who also attended up through April of this year. It was a way for me to grow professionally in my practice as a nurse. For him, it was a way to keep himself in a positive healing environment while living with a cancer diagnosis. I started nine months ago, thinking I would be able to support Michael while taking a deeper look at my own wellness. As it turned out, I ended up exploring the nuances of how to heal a broken heart.

During class this week, I spent the first couple of days thinking and talking about the impact of grief on all areas of my life. Only near the end, when I was tired of thinking anymore, did I finally start feeling, and then I couldn't stop crying. I cried many months' worth of tears, as I was held by this sacred community that had walked with us both through the last year of Michael's life. They too were grieving.

They grieved and they wanted to connect with me. I was touched by them reaching out but at times I felt overwhelmed by their need to share with me every experience they had of either remembering Michael or feeling his presence. From the sounds of it, Michael was very present this week, either in form or in the consciousness of the many he'd touched this last year through his courage and authenticity. So many people came up to me with a message they received from Michael during this week; things he told them or things he wanted to tell me from the other side. By the end of the week, I was exhausted from all of the input. I was exhausted because I don't really know if it's possible to communicate with those who have passed on.

I say I don't know, but I had an interesting experience in class a couple of months before Michael died that causes me to wonder. I was sitting next to my friend Karen, whose father had passed about three days before. We were starting a meditation, and as I closed my eyes, a vision appeared in my mind of a man standing in front of me. I wasn't afraid at first, as the image was very peaceful, but it also had an urgent quality. There were no actual words but it was as if he was trying to get my attention and needed to communicate something. I panicked. I told him inwardly to hold on while I went inside for a moment. I centered myself in loving and in every aspect of Spirit that I knew. As I did this, he patiently waited. When I looked up in my mind, he told me he needed me to tell Karen, his daughter, he was there for her. He then showed me an image of a little girl riding a tricycle by a pool while he sat in the background on a lawn chair. He told me she needed to know he loved her, and he was there for her that day. I wanted to ask questions, to find out more, but he looked at me, smiled, and was gone.

I was terrified. Nothing like this had ever happened to me in my life. After the lecture, I approached Karen with much hesitancy. I told her what had transpired and asked if she wanted to know what he wanted me to pass on, even though I wasn't sure it was real. She said yes, and I told her the story and shared with her the image and message. When she heard the details, she wept. She told me she had a picture of that exact scene at home. She said she was at peace with her father's passing, but the little girl part of her needed his presence.

I was speechless.

I was even more speechless when, later that day, she showed me a picture of her father, and it was the exact man who showed up in my mind and asked to communicate.

I chalked this whole experience up to a special circumstance and it faded into my memory. It faded until the moment people started coming to me with messages from Michael. Some resonated, some didn't, but in general I saw them as messages of love. I saw them as possibly real, but also possibly mixed up in the consciousness of the ether that brings us the reassurance we need each and every moment to go on.

I talked to my friend Susan about it, and how odd it felt to have so many people so sure they had a clear message from the other side. She lightened the whole thing up by wondering if I might treat them all as Elvis impersonators. I laughed out loud. I could see the tag line of "Elvis has left the building," and suddenly I saw all the messages as pure love and inspiration from Michael. He touched those people, each and every one of them. And whether he touched them in another realm, I will never know, but he touched their consciousnesses deeply enough that something did come through: the messages we most need to hear and the messages of loving reassurance that all is well. Reassurance that someone can live on forever in the hearts of those who love them, simply by the depth to which they inspired love.

I don't know about communication after death. There is much I do not know. I take comfort in the not-knowing, because then the answer can be whatever I need it to be in the moment. It can be a message of loving. It can be a brush of wind across my face or the light shining through the trees. It can be a feeling of him holding me when I need to be held. A conversation I can have when a big decision looms. Does it need to be substantiated in order to be comforting or useful? Do we ever really die when we have lived so clearly in one another's heart?

I saw an Elvis impersonator later that evening, walking on the boardwalk on the Santa Monica pier. I tried to catch up to him to see if he was real, but he disappeared into the crowd and left me only with Elvis's song, "Love me Tender" running through my head.

Friday, August 10th

I'm grateful today for the resilient voice within that encourages me to get up in the morning.

I'm grateful for Lucas's gymnastics program, and the small amount of determination I had to stay on task to get a birthday party scheduled for him there next week. I can ignore my upcoming birthday, but my boy is turning seven, and I'm grateful arranging his party turned out to be so easy.

I'm grateful for the Olympics, and the grace in which the evenings are filled with inspiration and entertainment.

I'm grateful for bike paths, and a kids' biking adventure that took me out of my head and into my body today.

I'm grateful for my mom, who is an absolute rock.

I'm grateful for our compassionate vet, and the hope that Alta's allergies will eventually settle down.

I'm grateful for the encouragement to keep writing even when I don't feel like writing.

I'm grateful for the awareness that grief will happen but wallowing is a choice.

This is hard today.

I feel like my words are incoherent and my gratitude is a stretch. But I'm persevering and trying to remember to slow down so that I don't get too overwhelmed. Stacks of paper and mail lie everywhere, all over the counter and table. Toys are everywhere. Laundry is stacked high and my bag has yet to be unpacked. But my boy is well loved and my dog is recovering. I had time to sit in the sun for a minute or two and my feet are slowly getting back under me as I adjust once again to what it means to come home.

I am back into my responsibilities with soft, fresh eyes, but the contrast to the single focus of healing I had while away at school is a challenge to navigate. I can do one thing at a time. I can get through one moment at a time. I can do one day at a time. The words "I don't know" are still the best answer to most questions people ask about what I am going to do. As far as I'm aware, nothing is an emergency. If I can reach this fall, I can get some room for my head. For now, I can take some room for my heart.

Sunday, August 12th

At the risk of sounding ungrateful for all the sympathy cards I received over the last couple of months, I am incredibly grateful today for birthday cards. My birthday is coming up, and there is a wonderful flow of cards and happy wishes coming through my mailbox. I first noticed them when I came home from California last week; a few cards in the midst of the bills. My heart felt heavy when I saw them, thinking they were more reminders of what has been lost. But when I opened them, they transformed my day with thoughts of abundance, joy, and encouragement to indulge in the sweetness of life. What a blessing! Instead of condolences, they address the subtle shift in my heart towards life.

I don't know how my actual birthday will go or what might come forward in missing Michael. He was such a genius with birthdays. For now, I'm grateful for the reminder that I'm indeed alive and able to enjoy the love available through friends, family, and a celebration of my birth. I'm also aware that left to my own devices, I would have skipped my birthday. Perhaps I would have bought myself a latte and gone for an extra long walk, but I would have left out thoughts of flowers, cards, or a nice dinner, as it would be too painful.

But now these cards are sweet reminders, standing upright on the counter next to a bouquet a precious friend gave me yesterday. The cards greet me when I come down the stairs each morning, reminding me to

"Indulge," "Enjoy every detail," "Be good to yourself," and to "Take in the sunshine, smiles, and love." These are the subtle messages I want to hear as I make my way back into the world from the depths of grief. These cards are a real gift. I have an urge to create cards with beautiful quotes that contrast with the normal line of condolence messages. I'm not sure what my calling is in life, but I suddenly have the awareness that I might be able to create a damn good line of bereavement cards . . . .

Wednesday, August 15th

I'm grateful today for an amazingly talented and compassionate dentist. I adore her, and am glad she does great work with minimal energetic invasiveness. When I went to get my teeth cleaned last week, I had a feeling I might have a cavity or two after the stress and intensity of the last six months. I have good teeth in general; healthy gums and a straight smile, but stress seems to break my teeth down like nothing else. Sigh!

Today I went in to have the first of two cavities filled, and I was anxious well beyond my normal going-to-the dentist anxiety. Perhaps it was because I spent the morning on the phone trying to figure out how the heck to roll over an inherited 401K. Or maybe it was spending the afternoon at an urban water feature with Lucas and eight hundred other children. Either way, it certainly wasn't the relaxed preparatory day I'd hoped for before dental work.

But the minute I sat down in the chair I felt cared for and nurtured instead of my expected emotions of terror and anxiety. As she gently worked on me, a wave of gratitude washed over. I thought how rare it is to feel cared for in teeth, mind, and soul while in the dental chair. I'm sure most dentists do care, but I never noticed before because I was so distracted by the drill in their hands. Today was different, and I understood she wanted to make this easy for me. I'm incredibly grateful.

Friday, August 17th

I'm grateful for metaphors and my ability to see something happening in the outside world and how it is playing out in my own life.

Lucas and I had gone to the beach for a couple days of camping and a change of scenery, and as we made our way home, we encountered a backup on the road that extended for miles. Word travelled from car to car that there had been a fatal accident ahead. I said a prayer for the persons involved and then set about figuring out whether to wait for the road to clear or to turn around and try to find another way home.

I chose to turn around and take another route instead of bumping up energetically against a barrier that was sure to take hours. The drive home took two hours longer than our usual route. We wound our way down the coast and then back through a valley an hour south of home. We got lost a couple of times, but there was a soothing feeling to the movement and to the dusk fading into night as we made our way in completely new territory.

I saw our diversion as a metaphor for not trying to push through the blocked road or go back to the beach and wait it out, but for choosing instead to find a new way home. In a way, it is symbolic of us no longer pursuing a future as a family that is no longer available—of not going back to the past and hiding in the grief of all that is lost—but instead choosing the confusion, unknown, and surprising beauty of a new path.

Monday, August 20th

This morning I remembered there's not much that can't be taken care of, or at least helped, by a good walk. My dad used to call it "*Solvitunido ambulando*," a quote in Latin that translates as "It is solved by walking."

I woke up in a funk again today, feeling like once again I was just going through the motions. Get up, feed the dog, make tea, meditate, do yoga, check email, snuggle with kiddo, make breakfast...check, check, check...all emotionless. Unless the emotion completely floors me. In which case I cry until I can once again get up and go through the motions.

It's not a terrible rhythm to be in right now, and I'm being gentle with myself. I know that at least I'm getting out of bed and taking care of everything that needs to be taken care of at this time. It's okay that I'm not feeling engaged and joyful, and it's okay that the sadness is intensely overwhelming.

I just need to keep on keeping on until little bits of joy make their way in between the yoga poses, the meals, the steps of each walk. And today the walking helped. A change of scenery, a deep breath amongst the forest trees, a chance to see a horizon vaster than my backyard. My steps that were heavy as I left the house had a little more spring when I returned an hour later, and I remembered that a walk always helps.

Michael knew how good walking was for me and when I got myself worked up about anything, particularly if it was going to involve him needing to get worked up as well, he would encourage me to take a long walk. In the beginning of our relationship, I was a little offended when he sent me off walking, as if it was an admission I was worked up and irrational. Over time, I realized it was an invitation to take the high road, to find my ground instead of buying into whatever drama my mind was creating. It was a chance for my feet to take me toward peace.

Everything is better after a walk. If nothing else, the dog is happy and exercise can be checked off the list of things to do. But there is something more subtle as well, some softening of the mind and heart after being lulled by the rhythm of stepping through the morning with purpose, rather than undirected energy.

The walking today helped and for this I am grateful.

Thursday, August 23rd

Every once in a while, in the midst of grief and confusion, a seemingly angelic intervention comes along, and suddenly everything feels right again, even if for only a moment. I had one of those moments today, and the gratitude runs deep.

We are on a road trip, checking out the Oregon landscape, running from grief under the guise of looking for interesting places to live someday. I'm well aware that road trips now are a handy illusion; that if I go away, then maybe when I get back home everything will have been an awful dream. Michael will be there waiting for me. I know it's not true, but there's still that slight wedge of freedom opening my heart out on the road; a sense of adventure that can only be had when home has the solidity of my beloved waiting to welcome me back.

Today, driving out from Crater Lake, taking in its full majesty followed by a stunning drive through the gorge carved by the Rogue River, I was free and happy. But then an awareness struck me—blindsided me really—that when I got home I wouldn't be telling Michael about all the beauty. Emptiness hit hard, and although there was still much wonder to be seen, the day took on a bittersweet feel. The feel stayed with me until we reached the home of my mom's friends who live just outside of Ashland and along the Rogue River. We found ourselves on the banks of the river in the midst of a joy-filled home that was welcoming to dogs, playful with my sweet child, and even had a pasture full of grazing horses.

The setting was beautiful, and yet what truly struck me was the kindness and love that met us at the door. One of the first questions my mom's friend Mary asked me was, "What is it that nurtures you now?" All I could say, looking at the beauty of their land, was, "This. All of this." I knew I was in the presence of an angel and her family. For one evening, we took in all the love available to us and I felt completely blessed to be alive. We tucked into a family full of joy and a land full of animals, all thriving in the sun on a few acres on the river. I needed a blessing today, and one was delivered. I am so incredibly grateful.

Sunday, August 26th

A dull ache has set in these days; there's a feeling of grief more like a shadow than a full-on wave. It must be how chronic pain feels after the acute crisis is over and the patient is back home. They're caring for themselves without the support and intervention they had during their hospital stay. Their urge to allow the dull ache to take over might be nearly insurmountable. Grief feels this way for me now. I'm going through the motions, wearing a cloak of ache. I feel joy, I do everything I'm supposed to be doing, even take trips and have fun, but there is this underlying ache that permeates everything. It catches in my throat every once in a while, and a small sob escapes that never quite gets going full-bore.

I'm grateful that I'm not completely laid out with anxiety. I'm functioning in the world, parenting and taking care of bills, planning outings and putting off questions that just won't go away. "Why did this happen?" "Did this really happen?" "Is he near in some way?" "Why me?" Questions that up until now I haven't had time to process because they hurt too damn much. Now that I see time without him stretching out before me, I feel even more deeply the wonderment of how any of this ever happened.

Life is going on, with me or without me, and for this moment, I am left behind simply for a lack of interest. I am going through the motions necessary to stay on the train, but I'm certainly not aware what destination my ticket is marked for. I'm here for the ride until I can make some kind of clear decision of where to go from here.

Monday, August 27th

I had a near miss with a migraine this morning. I'm grateful for strong coffee, Tylenol, and the barometer of a migraine aura to remind me that times have been stressful. It's a good idea to slow down, release emotions, and be more gentle with myself.

Tuesday, August 28th

So much heaviness and sadness has enveloped me the last few days, so today I'm grateful I finally got a break in the emotional weather. Last night I was so disappointed after a miscommunication left me in the park, expecting to walk with friends after setting up childcare, and then I realized I had the wrong night. I was sad to miss the comfort of walking with my women friends, but it in the end it gave me an excuse to watch a beautiful sunset and sink into a good cry.

So today I tried again. I set up childcare and met them in the park for a walk. I'm grateful I rallied to meet them again. The deliciousness of friendship was nourishing, and the laughter flowed. I'm grateful for amazing women friends and the blessings of connection. There was a full moon and we walked in the magical time where evening turns to night. Our deep conversation ranged from sacred to laughter. For this I am grateful.

September

"There is nothing wrong with grief. Grief itself is an aspect of love. Let it be as it is. Be humbled by it. Then it is a great teacher."

– Gangaji

Wednesday, September 5th

It's been a while since I've written. Not because I'm not grateful, but because there isn't much in it that feels profound. Tonight something shifted though, and several pieces that have been rambling around in my head started to become coherent.

It began when I came home with Lucas this afternoon and heard from a friend that a relative of hers had gotten bad news about her cancer spreading. My friend was upset and needed to talk. I listened, and even though I responded in an attentive way to the challenge of her situation, I realized I was holding it differently than my friend. Her take on the situation was that everything was terrible. Things were going downhill and it was truly a tragedy. While all that flowed through me as well, some deeper part of me knew that no matter what happened with the relative's cancer, she was going to be okay and so was my friend. Not "okay" in a way that everything would turn out the way we wanted it to, but "okay" in the sense that no matter what happened it was all going to be okay—even if the relative actually died and her family and friends had to live the pain of grief.

This awareness came as if I was a child seeing a new toy for the first time. As if it was a bright, shiny thing to explore and wonder at before touching it and examining it more closely. Underneath everything I'm feeling right now—the unknowing, the pain of grief, the challenge of single parenting, the loss of shared dreams—I recognize a complete and unbreakable wholeness. Now that is something to be grateful for. I have witnessed and lived the very real tragedy my friend is so afraid of and found that on the other side there is still wholeness and possibility.

Later, on the way to choir for the first time since Michael died, I listened to The Wailin' Jenny's song "Things That You Know." As I was driving and singing along I was struck by the lyrics, which said, "There are things that you know, from where you've had to go, maybe soon you'll find a place to call your own."

And I realized I was there. I was home within it all.

The journey through places I've had to go, even when I didn't want to, has brought me to a place of knowing, and is an incredible gift. I now know there's a wholeness underlying all things. I knew that in the moment of Michael's death, and I do my best to remember that now as I walk through grief.

I've been philosophizing and thinking quite a bit about existentialism lately, because in a way, I'm trying to figure out who I am now that Michael is gone. I feel like I'm in an odd void after touching something so sacred and I'm unsure how to be in the world. However, the one thing I do know is that I want to be more loving. I want to live from that loving in a way that makes small irritations unremarkable. Somewhere within me, I am moved and led by love in a way that is a result of suffering but has forever changed my life.

Walking through the journey of Michael's illness and death created a space for loving and contemplation that endures long afterwards. I don't know if I could have understood this without having gone with him right to the door of the infinite. His passing changed me, and though I would give anything to have had a different outcome, I do know I will always be grateful for the gift of his loving that was magnified in how we walked together through the end of his life. He took me to the place where everything really is okay, despite any outcome, and there is a place of rest in that infinite loving.

Friday, September 7th

This week I've finally had time to breathe. On Tuesday Lucas started school again for the fall, and I think both of us were grateful for a return to a consistent routine. I've had time to reflect, lots of time to cry, and a moment here and there to feel like I'm making a dent in all the paperwork and bills that have been piling up in my office. I tried to keep Lucas busy this summer, but probably was a little on the manic side, filling the time with road trips, visits to the science museum, parks, and play-dates. It may have been better for him to have more unstructured time, but the busyness helped ease the burden of the long hours at home, just the two of us. I've been doing my best to be present as a mom, which has meant many things have fallen through the cracks. But we made it to fall, and the shift into a semblance of a rhythm feels good.

This week he seems to be thriving back in school, and it's a relief for me to have time to grieve without worrying about how it will impact him. I know it's good to model how to express all these feelings, but it's challenging to know how much or what to express when he seems to not be exhibiting a lot of grief. For the most part, he's doing quite well, with only the occasional welling of emotion when he realizes Michael isn't here and possibly isn't coming back. I can see that part of him thinks this is temporary, and his young mind can't quite grasp the fullness of what has happened. Unlike me, who feels such a variety of emotions around not only the present loss, but also our future together, Lucas is more in the moment and therefore grieves in the moment. He isn't yet caught off-guard as I am by the sudden realization that his dad won't be there for his first baseball game, but instead is touched by grief in the moment when he wants to play Legos or have Michael read to him as their normal bedtime routine. His grief is in the moment in comparison to the persistent fog that follows me through my days.

I do know he was relieved to have me back after so much of my time was committed to caring intensely for Michael in the last month of his life. I also know that the most important thing I can do for him right now is to take care of myself so I can be present for him. His biggest fear right now is something happening to me, and that fear is how his grief is expressing itself at this time—as a fear of me leaving him as well. I know his grief is likely to emerge more strongly at some point, and for now I'm grateful for the comfort of routine supporting him in a way that a free-floating summer of jumbled emotion didn't quite do.

Saturday, September 8th

Some days I'm struck by the gratitude that comes forward in odd little moments and connections. I was at wit's end yesterday with Alta. She has seasonal allergies and has been suffering with red and raw paws, itchy ears, and an appearance that's overall pitiful in nature. She looks absolutely miserable.

Earlier today, when I sat down to put ointment between the pads of her paws to soothe the itching, I came across a matted, sticky, black substance. Tar? Pitch? I almost burst into tears at the addition of this to her already sore paws as I tried in vain to cut it off. Then in a flash of memory I thought to myself, "Butter!" The gas attendant who cleaned my windshield the other day told me the only thing he couldn't get off was a spot of sap right in my line of sight. I asked him what to do, and he said "Butter." "Butter?" It turns out butter is the magic substance for dissolving all things toxic and thick without countering it with another toxic substance. I certainly wasn't going to put paint thinner on Alta's feet, so I figured butter was a win-win solution in that it would either work, or, if it didn't, it would be a nice treat for her to lick.

The butter was magic, and for this I am grateful. The gooey mass of pitch dissolved between my fingers as I slathered her tender paw with globs of butter. I had that sweet rush of gratitude for the gas station attendant who was kind enough to share his wisdom. It was a small thing, originally intended to fix a small problem on a windshield, but it turned into so much more. It turned into the thing today that helped me to trust that the world is indeed a friendly place. That when I most need help and am at the end of my coping ability, something comes through to catch me.

Today it was butter for an already challenged allergic dog paw. Tomorrow, I can only guess that it will be something just as miraculous. That it will remind me to keep going, to keep looking for the good even when all seems lost.

Wednesday, September 12th

I'm grateful for New Seasons Market and the little boost of inspiration and creativity I received while shopping today. I have to admit that I haven't been to the store much lately. My mom has been keeping us stocked with the basics and I haven't felt much like cooking anything extravagant or elegant. But my mom went home to Alaska yesterday, and for dinner, Lucas and I were back to our standard quesadillas with a few cut-up veggies and avocado.

Today I have friends from out of town coming for dinner and I want to do a bit more than barely get by. It's not just any friend; it's my writing teacher who I haven't seen in over ten years and is now relatively famous. Although I'm sure she would understand if I made us all quesadillas, there's just something about a writer that makes me want to get creative.

So in honor of my dinner guests, I went to the store in search of a red onion and some pumpkin seeds to fancy up a kale salad. What I found when I got there was a renewed interest in shopping for good food, which inspired me to cook. I talked to the wine guy and discovered a great Oregon white. I sampled cheese, found my favorite hors d'oeuvre cracker, and bought a little dark chocolate to get me through any afternoon slump. When I left, I had an amazing menu planned, wine to pair with the halibut I had defrosting in the fridge, and my soul was ready to put on an apron. When I got in the car and realized I felt good about cooking, I promptly began to cry. Tears of gratitude for guests who make it worth planning a nice dinner, tears of sadness remembering how Michael and I had so much fun entertaining but tonight I was on my own, and tears of resignation about moving on and out into my life without him.

I miss him every day and still can't believe he's gone. Yet entertaining on my own, making plans to fill evenings that could otherwise be so empty and stretch out for years ahead, and wondering where my life is going, all create a reality that I'm building a new life out of the wreckage of tragedy. I miss him. My son misses him. We talk about it, but we also don't talk about it. The days blend together and the moments move on and we do our best to stay in the present, inspired or sad, living the life to which we have been called. God bless us.

Friday, September 14th

Today, I've been a bit of a mess. Not in a bad way, as I know eventually I'll have to cry every tear, but in a sense of breaking down at just about everything. I don't want to even leave the house.

I had to go to the DMV today, which on its own is a good reason to cry even without grief. I had to change the title on our car to my name only, so I can sell it to pay off our other car and reduce my monthly expenses. I knew I needed to do this, but the whole damn thing just seemed unfair. As I drove off from the house, the finality of the task sunk in. It made us a one-car family now, and that just seemed all too real for me. We don't need two cars because Michael isn't coming back. I probably didn't make it better with the CD playing in the car from the last Portland Peace Choir concert. It has songs that get right to my core, and one of the ones that played, "For the Beauty of the Earth," was the same one the choir sang at Michael's memorial service. In an uncanny turn of events, that song came on just as I passed the funeral home that took care of his cremation. I sobbed as I drove by, remembering taking care of all the details. I remembered the kind funeral home director, and the way that I had never before noticed there was a funeral home right along a major street near our house. Today it seemed lit up in neon colors amidst the flood of memories.

I know I need to cry every tear.

At the DMV I was numb as I processed all the paper-work. I could tell the solemn attendant felt bad when I gave him Michael's license and death certificate with the vehicle registration and he told me I couldn't have the license back. I must have looked incredulous, because at the end of all the paperwork he punched a hole to make the license invalid and said, "You look like a really nice lady, so I'm going to give this back to you for your memories, but no one sees this, okay?"

I took it gratefully and tucked it into my wallet behind my driver's license, knowing in some strange way it represented parts of him that couldn't be taken from me. Strange, but oddly comforting, and I cried there in gratitude for the attendant's kindness on this ever-so-challenging day of completion.

Wednesday, September 19th

I received an email from *Oprah Magazine* about the possibility of being published in the December issue. I felt immense gratitude for the power of taking small steps towards my dream of being a writer. If it's published, it will be short, but maybe the universe is telling me that, yes, I need to be writing. I need to put my work out there, and the stories that need to be heard will be picked up.

It was a blessed relief after having had such a hard day. I cried all morning to the point of dehydration. I finally mustered up the energy to meet someone for lunch, and when I walked out to my car afterwards, I got the email about the magazine. I laughed and cried all at the same time and felt the nature of hope moving me back out into the world.

Thursday, September 20th

Okay, this task was a big one. I just finished rebooking the trip to Hawaii—Michael's bucket list trip that we never got to take. We were supposed to go last April, and in rebooking the tickets, I remembered all the energy he had for the trip. He and Leit took Lucas over to buy snorkel gear and talked about the trip endlessly while the rest of us wondered if it was a wise idea. My mom and I had slaved away at our computers for hours last spring, trying to get halfway reasonable tickets using companion fares and pooling all of our mileage awards together. We ended up booking them from Seattle instead of Portland, just to make it more doable, and a few days later the whole trip fell through when the hospice nurse said he needed to be more stable to travel. Hell, I knew that.

You see, airplanes and advanced lung metastasis don't go well together. The weekend before, he had struggled with a day trip to Hood River. I wondered on that day how I would get him on the plane to Hawaii and back. All he would have been able to do in Hawaii would be to sit at the condo, while I tried to keep Lucas happy and simultaneously worry about him back at the condo. Sigh. We never went. The hospice nurse was worried he would die on the way over or while he was there, and she didn't want us to deal with the aftermath of such a situation. It all seemed so doable at the time—and hell, why not die in Hawaii? But now, afterwards, I see how incredibly complex and impossible the whole thing would have been. In the end we bought some Hawaiian beer, listened to Jack Johnson's *Kakura Festival* CD, and watched a slideshow of Leit's girlfriend's trip to Hawaii. We all smiled, but inside we ached for what was lost.

So today, I booked the bucket list trip so we can fulfill Michael's dream of taking his little boy snorkeling. We'll go in March, and I trust that by then we'll be able to meet the trip with renewed energy and enough happiness to enjoy being together and remembering Michael without being completely flattened by grief.

But the point of today's gratitude is not that we're going, but for how amazing the agent was on the phone. My mom had been round and round with the airlines after we cancelled last spring; getting dates changed, fares refunded, tickets held, and promises of decreased change fees. But today, the woman on the phone was totally clear the minute I told her what had happened and what I needed to do. She moved with Bruce Lee clarity, carving away at the complexity of name changes, companion fares, and rebooking fees.

When it was done, the agent told me she didn't think it was possible, but she was going to try to get her supervisor to waive all the change fees as a onetime thing, considering our circumstances. I wasn't too optimistic, as we were already beyond what a normal airline would do for us. They had been great to us twice already, and I just wanted our trip all squared away. She came back and said we were all clear and there were no fees. I thanked her for her compassion and clarity. She replied by saying she had buried her mother in Hawaii not too many years ago, and it was the least she could do for us.

Bless her and her kindness. I am grateful and humbled by the ways in which loss brings us together, forever moving toward a world of peace and compassion.

Sunday, September 23rd

I'm not sure why I thought I could bypass the depths of grief. I think I figured that because I've worked so much in hospice care and studied psychology that I wouldn't have to go through the deep, dark spaces of grief myself. I wouldn't have to watch the bad television. I wouldn't have the one too many glasses of wine. I wouldn't have to have the days of wearing sweat pants and crying on the couch while the dog stares longingly at the door for a walk.

I suppose thinking I would miss all this would be like orthopedic surgeons believing they wouldn't have to have their own compound fractures set. Or gynecologists not needing annual pap smears. I have to grieve right along with the rest of those who have lost loved ones. Despite my work experience in end-of-life and psychology, my emotions, thoughts, and physical place in this world have completely changed. My body is healing. My heart is healing. But it will take time for them to become whole again.

Gratitude is still here. Mostly for the awareness. For the awareness that trying to go through grief without actually feeling grief is a farce; that one glass of wine makes things feel a little better and three makes them feel worse; that one episode of Grey's Anatomy helps turn off my brain before I go to sleep and three episodes makes it hard to wake up in the morning because I went to bed at midnight.

I'm still taking care of myself. Gently watching the process. Holding myself with the part of me that knows underneath it will all be okay. And when I can't hold myself, finding a friend to hold me.

Monday, September 24th

I was completely thrown off yesterday, when a well-meaning friend of Michael's said she knew someone who loved our house and did I want to talk with him about selling? She thought it was fabulous they might be interested in buying, and seemed genuinely shocked when my response was to cry.

I cried because, while I know I need to sell my house, it seemed all too real and all too soon. I know she meant it out of love and was trying to help. But couldn't she see it was way too much for me? That to bring it up at all would trigger my instability? Me knowing I need to sell my house is one thing, but someone else trying to help me sell it feels rushed. Strange nuances, I know.

The situation reminded me of when my dad was diagnosed with brain cancer ten years ago. I gave up my apartment in Boulder to move back to Alaska to be closer to him. I loved that apartment. It had a view of the Flatirons and acres of open space surrounded me. It was where I was going to launch my writing career. I had taken a few months off of work, and with a view of the blue sky and mountains, I wrote each morning, a steaming cup of coffee at my desk. Every afternoon I then went for a hike. When I let that apartment go it was as if all my dreams went with it. The pain of moving, even though I wouldn't have chosen differently, was excruciating.

A friend of mine scored that apartment after I tipped her off I was moving. It infuriated me. She didn't do anything wrong. She just moved into an amazing apartment. But I directed my anger at her, as if she had robbed me of not only my apartment, but my dreams too. I should have been happy for her, but I don't think we ever spoke again.

Today, I know that the friend of Michael's was acting out of love when she offered to introduce me to a potential buyer for our house. But I'm not ready to think about selling my house. I live here now. I live here with all our dreams wrapped tightly around me, wishing they weren't going to shatter.

Tuesday, September 25th

I made it through today, our anniversary. It was actually easier than yesterday. Despite my wanting to be completely alone, I ended up surrounded with love. I was held by two dear friends over a video conference; given the gift of a massage by one of the most talented massage therapists I know, who even sent me home with a vase full of flowers; and ended the afternoon sitting on the porch with my dear friend Annie, having a glass of wine while the dogs and kids played and we talked about how much we are like family.

I am so grateful for the way people show up, time after time, challenging my limiting beliefs about being alone in this world. We are not alone. We are loved and held, and all the rest is an illusion. It's funny how at times in my life when I felt abandoned by people, I turned to God to know I wasn't alone. And now, when I feel abandoned by God, people are there at every turn, holding me, loving me, carrying me, right into the arms of faith. I have faith now in a bigger love than I can hold myself and I don't care if it's God or human. All I know right now is that it's real. How could it not be real as I move through this day that would have marked our eighth year together and somehow remain whole?

Wednesday, September 26th

I've been reflecting today on helping out my friend Hillary by volunteering for an event she's coordinating for her visiting spiritual teacher. It's as if I've been swept up in a beautiful current that's magically moving to some sort of culmination and healing. Not necessarily for me, but by helping I've become an integral part of it, and engaging today made me feel alive.

I imagined myself having a conversation with this teacher so I could thank her for the answer she gave when Hillary asked her a couple of months ago about the anxiety I had experienced following Michael's death. Her guidance and reassurance about being gentle with myself was so comforting. My understanding was that she recognized the anxiety and the importance of taking time to ease back into the day-to-day workings of the world after such a sacred and intimate experience of being with a dying loved one. In her response, she seemed to honor how being so close to death, so close to the moment of his passing, brought forth a remarkable sacredness that has changed me forever. What came forward as I imagined this conversation with her was that I want to live in a way that honors the moment of his death. All I want to do is show up in a way that honors that moment. I want to show up for my friends, my child, myself. I want to trust that as I show up in integrity and honoring of complete pure love and authenticity, the larger cosmos of loving will meet me in that place with clarity and grace. That's all I want to do.

I want to live in this way because I know what an incredible gift I received by being so close to Michael at the time of his death. I have been present to many deaths in my work as a hospice nurse, but to be so close with Michael was a different experience all together. As he was dying, I felt his fear as if it was my own. I sat with him through more suffering than either of us ever imagined anyone could bear. I felt the love that surrounded us. My dreams were melded with his dreams, full of angels and a vast loving, and I would wake incredulous to find him still there next to me, hanging on to this life. In his last week I endured so much but at the same time was so clearly aware of the sacredness of life. Everything unimportant fell away, and there was nothing left but love. And in that last breath, the thing I felt usher him to the other side was full of a love that was breathtaking and stunning in nature. Everything fell away, everything, and all that was left was love.

There was love in a human sense—for Michael, and between all the friends and family that were here to help—but there was something more. There was an overarching presence of love outside of me that I want to remember for the rest of my life. It is a love that is present and available no matter what we're going through, or how completely beyond our limits we are functioning. It is a love that I want to remember as being always available and more important than any tangible thing on this earth. If I can live remembering this broader love, then I will never be alone, I will always have access to a different way of being in the world, and to a place to source from for kindness when I bump up against a world that isn't always kind.

I feel as though I am living in a place just beyond my usual human perception, that perhaps the veil between this world and whatever is beyond is still slightly open. The tangible nature of the day-to-day still touches me, but it is surrounded by knowing that beyond anything I can experience here is something greater, even more loving and compassionate, in which I can trust beyond any joy or suffering of this human life. I have lived this in faith, but now I feel as if I am living it from a place of knowing. I trusted before that love is the essence of God, but being so intimately close in Michael's death, I was able to have this love touch me as if I too had walked through that door of beckoning light. I feel the blessing of that touch, and if I continue to live in such a way that remembers that blessing, then I have received the one gift that lies inside of this monumental loss.

October

"The grief wave moves through, sometimes as if the whole ocean is emptying itself over me, but it does not last forever. The grief wave does not last forever."

Tuesday, October 2nd

What once was daily writing is now weekly. Gratitude is still present, and it shows up in so many ways that it's swept up with the pace of life. I'm being pulled along by an underground current. Whether I make steps forward or not, I am somehow carried.

Which brings me to talk of faith. I want to write about faith and how it came up for me in conversation with my friend Carrie, who is coaching me through this first year of grief. I'm so grateful she has carved out an hour each week to be my companion on this journey of grieving. We spoke of faith today in relation to my questioning and wondering. I think there is a part of me, or better yet, I know there is a part of me that is questioning my faith. It is the place from which anger, bitterness, and resentment arise. It is a place I know must be explored, for it feels far more dangerous unattended to, gathering strength in the darkness.

I am afraid that I am losing faith. I am afraid that as I go through these darkest and most challenging days of my life, my lack of attention to meditation, to prayer, to self-care, to self-respect, is somehow jeopardizing my ability to be a faithful and spiritual person.

I feel that if I let go of faith, or if I somehow lose my faith, then I won't be safe or protected in the world. But how can I feel faithful, protected, safe in the world after what has happened? Michael was my safety, the physical manifestation of my protection. He even protected me from my own critical words. He held me, loved me, and protected me, energetically, physically, emotionally, and socially, whenever I didn't have the energy to do it for myself. Having lost him I feel abandoned, and my faith is shaken.

Which causes me to question what kind of faith I actually hold stock in. Have I had faith in a God, in a universal love, that is outside of myself and is supposed to protect me from bad things happening?

Bad things did happen—if we want to divide things into good and bad. If faith is the harbinger of good, and lack of faith is the scourge of all things bad, then I must have lacked the faith to prevent Michael's death. Talk about a load of guilt.... Is it possible at age forty-four, with all the seeking, questioning, and learning in spirituality I have done, that there still lies within me a sense of faith as childlike as this?

I know better. I have lived better. I have lived through the fires of suffering and I know there is no faith that can protect me from the pain. There is only a larger faith that can walk with me through suffering in a way that somehow finds learning and growth in the path.

I want to live in this kind of faith. I want to live in a faith that trusts God is with me no matter what happens in my life and no matter what I do in my life. If I chant forward or backward, or sit just so, or follow a particular religious path, it does not matter. All that matters is that I trust that my soul, my essence, is held in pure love. I can have faith in loving. I can trust that if I am in a space of loving, I am whole no matter what transpires in the physical world.

I want to let go of the faith that is an illusion of protection; that which can only be with me in safety and in what I determine to be good in my life. The other kind of faith, the faith I know I need to live in, is within. This faith trusts that no matter what happens, I will have the strength, the grace, and above all, the gratitude for this simple life, no matter what is asked. This is a faith in which I can place my trust. Down at the root, it is the faith that cannot be shattered.

Wednesday, October 3rd

I'm grateful for something being easy.

I sold my car today. I sold my car today without re-alizing my worst fear of having to test-drive it with a hundred slimy guys contacting me off Craigslist. I sold my car today without manifesting any of my fears about haggling and worrying and fretting and eventually tak-ing it to a dealer because I can't handle the stress. I sold my car today, because it's damn time that something came easy.

I sold my car to a friend of a friend who was looking for my exact car. I sold my car to a woman who was just as overwhelmed at buying a car as I was at selling one. No haggling, only over-acquiescence that only could be done by two women wanting to make sure everything was okay for the other person. Michael must have laughed on the other side, shaking his head at the incredible grace and flow that meets me in the places where I should need hard facts and a hard edge. He never did see why I be-lieve trust and acquiescence can be easier than that hard edge. And today, thank God, they were.

I sold my car and there is a grace in the air that helps me to believe that everything, all the looming decisions, could be so easy, and all I have to do is set the intention and wait for the flow to find me . . . .

Thursday, October 4th

I am grateful for the stunning and memorable clarity Michael had about assisted suicide. I have been reliving lately, at the undesirable hour of three in the morning, the days before his death; the suffering, the loss of dignity, the pain, the torturous times I would rather not have endured. I have been reliving those days, those hours, and questioning whether there was anything else I could have done. As if with the freedom of knowing there was nothing else I could have done it would all be easier. It is an illusion, but a worthy one.

As I relive those times, I find myself in an incredible place of gratitude for how clear Michael was about how he did not want to be taken to the other side of the veil by anything other than his own process. His oncologist, still choked up from telling us how far the cancer had spread, asked Michael about Death with Dignity as he was referring him to hospice care. Assisted suicide is legal here in Oregon. The oncologist explained to us it would take time, precious time we might not have, unless we put things into motion right away. Even though he was afraid, Michael was adamant he did not want assistance. He was afraid of his mechanism of death, the potential for suffocation, the fear of the pain that would indeed eventually envelope his whole being. And yet, even in the face of his physician offering relief from that very fear, he clearly, boldly, and unwaveringly answered that it was not an option for him.

I never questioned his reasoning. I knew it was a matter of faith for him and there was no reason to question it. And so now, in reliving the suffering and anguish at his death, I think of those last moments and how I cannot question myself either. I can only look back to the grace, the strength, and the clarity I had in following his wishes, and to the gratitude that he spoke them so clearly. May we all be as clear for our loved ones in giving this precious gift of awareness of our choices as we face whatever it is that will take us across that great river of light to the other side.

Friday, October 5th

The emptiness at times seems endless. I find myself drifting, unsure how to bring myself out of the river's current that is slowly pulling me away from any confidence I ever knew. I know I have to follow this current, let myself drift, let myself stray from believing that life could ever be the same without Michael. The dreams are different, the way of life is different, the parenting is different, and the weekends, the nights, and the days are all different. I want so desperately for them to feel the same; to even have the possibility they may one day be the same. But for now, the truth is they are different. I must live into a new life, one that is far away from the old one, the old dreams, the old way of being in the world.

Am I changed? Am I changed for good or for worse? I don't know what to do. I wander around in this too-big house and try to figure out a way to comfort myself, to keep busy, stay numb, and hold at bay the decisions I must make to unloose my soul from its attachment to a life that once was but is no more. I am still myself, but a different play has started and I'm playing the old role without a new script. Is there a new role? Or is there just me now, laid bare, waiting for life to begin again without a storyline, without the illusion that things can ever be anticipated, expected, or counted on? Is it possible to have a life that is simply in the moment?

Sunday, October 7th

This evening I had one of those frozen-in-time moments while Lucas was getting ready for bed. I was being an unusually patient parent, and even though I had told Lucas a thousand times to please just brush his teeth, followed by multiple requests for putting on his pajamas, I somehow found the grace to oblige when he asked me to sing a song he loves called "Bambelela." It's a traditional spiritual song from South Africa, and means never give up. He dances to its catchy tune even when it's just me singing instead of a whole choir. It always makes him smile, and for this reason I sang it again tonight for the one-hundredth time after the hundred other bedtime requests.

I sang for him in that moment. I sang in a moment that, on other nights, would have broken me and I would have pleaded with him to please just get in bed. But tonight I sang and he danced and smiled his little, happy smile, and time stopped. It stopped, and I saw myself observing his happiness. He was a little boy singing with his mom, adding some dance steps, and smiling a grin that only a seven-year-old losing his teeth can smile. In that moment, he was a happy little boy. Not a little boy whose dad had died. Not a little boy who needed protecting or coddling or extra attention, just a happy little boy getting ready for bed. And in that moment was my freedom. The freedom to be his mom. Not a mom who was parenting alone and overwhelmed by years of responsibility looming ahead. Not a mom who was exhausted and ready for a sliver of time to lay down and cry after a busy weekend. I was simply a mom singing to her little boy. A happy mom, singing a happy tune, and trusting in the translation of the words: *"Bambelela, bambelela, never give up, never give up."*

It is indeed my sweet little boy who keeps me from giving up. His bright, happy face asking me to sing or play is what keeps me going through so many days when I would rather stay in bed. It's a challenge to observe the authenticity of his happiness and how quickly he can shift from being completely overtaken by sadness one minute to humming while he brushes his teeth the next. But he reminds me there is something other than the pervasive grief I feel. His young life, extending out before us is a lifeline for me to be carried forward as well. There are times when he struggles, especially at night, when he's more afraid of the dark than he ever was before Michael died, and at those times I can pull him forward with a smile and a song. We balance each other out on this rocky path of loss, and together, we are finding our way.

Thursday, October 11th

I hadn't cried in a long time. Maybe a few tears here and there, but I was in need of a good, long cry. Today I finally let go and sobbed. Then I lay down on my office floor for a long time and breathed in the relief of acknowledging how tired I felt. I needed to know how tired I was and that it's okay to stop pushing, staying busy, distracting myself from the real feelings coming up.

I'm tired, and it's okay to lie down.

The next time I want it to be on a couch, but today it was good enough to lay on the carpet and sob until there were no more sobs left. I checked in, thinking there might have been residual tears in there somewhere, but for that moment they were clear.

In that space after crying, I finally breathed. I breathed, and everything that half an hour ago seemed so hard was now doable, or at least in the realm of a to-do list. For me, it's easier to be strong through all this. It is easier to show up and stuff it down and create the illusion, for myself and for others, that I can take this journey with a strength of heart like steel. It turns out though that my heart is not steel; my heart is human, and it hurts. But it is harder for me to cry than it is to cover it up. Until I break, that is. Then it's easier to cry for a while and then dust myself off and do the things that need to be done.

It would be good for me to remember in the build-up to the eventual breakdown that I always have more clarity when I give myself permission to cry. When I get over-whelmed with grief and wonder whether or not I even want to go on living, it would be wise to note how hopeful I eventually feel after I give myself the time and space to go into the grief rather than push it away. Learning to cry is perhaps the hardest part of this journey.

Friday, October 12th

The beauty of today is that when I woke up, I wasn't still on the floor. I wasn't crying anymore, and I had the energy to take Lucas to the pool. I made it through yesterday and I woke up into today. I met yesterday's deep hurt, met it fully, and now I have a different understanding. The grief wave does not last forever, even though it feels like it will last forever. The grief wave moves through, sometimes as if the whole ocean is emptying itself over me. And then it is gone. I am left standing on the beach, still whole, still alive, still here, functional and moving into this world. I am not moving away from the world I shared with Michael so much as I am moving into the life that is present for me now.

This is important, because I want to acknowledge that I was actually engaged in the process of living today. I had times today when I wasn't simply going through the motions to get through, to get one day closer to some illusionary time when grief might end, or to simply survive. I lived today, for most of the day, in the presence of full engagement.

I helped a friend organize a launch party for the radio show she is producing, and it turned out that by asking for my assistance, she was actually helping me. She gave me the opportunity to engage in work and to be part of something amazing. I showed up fully for the first time in a long time. And in order to show up fully, I had to be my essence, to be in flow, to be fully engaged, without doubt or fear over whether I was doing things right. This wasn't about me; it was about supporting someone I care about in doing something that was a big deal for her, and I showed up.

Here's where it gets tricky. The crux is all I truly did was show up in my loving. In that place of loving, I was teamed up with three incredibly attuned women, and we all worked to make the launch a success. At the end of the evening, we ended up talking about the nature of loving and what happens when you surrender to it fully.

When I got in my car to leave, I was surprised by suddenly feeling alone. And then I remembered that loving. When I called to check in on Lucas, who was having his first-ever sleepover with his best friend, I had a wave of wondering over what I would do with myself, going home to an empty house. And I remembered that loving again. As I pulled into traffic, I had a flash of wondering what if I was in an accident and this evening had sealed the last day with my child and my own precious life. I worried if it was my last evening on earth I should have been doing something else tonight. Then it hit me that it doesn't matter what I do as long as I am in my loving.

Tonight I was alive to how it feels to be of loving service. It wasn't grand in any outer way, but if it was the last night of my life and my little boy was happy with his friends, I would be complete. The invitation now is to have every moment feel complete by simply being love. I don't know how this will look. I know that it used to look like being "in love" more than it looked like "being love." My guess is it will look like a crazy kaleidoscope of unimagined manifestations and a whole cast of characters, some of whom I've yet to meet. It will be a tapestry of color, of feeling, of moving through the tragedies and celebrations of life. Most importantly, it will be full engagement in the awareness that I have one function in this life of being—living love.

Today I showed up in that loving, and I am grateful.

Sunday, October 14th

Today I'm aware of the opportunity to receive help and guidance from women who have raised children on their own. I have so many concerns about how to raise Lucas without Michael. He's an easygoing, happy kid, but I worry about whether I can give him everything he needs. Will I make the right decisions for him about schools, healthcare, and healthy limits for behavior? I've lost the person who I used to share all the parenting decisions with, and now I feel alone and always in need of advice.

Up until now, I've shied away from advice from single moms. Divorce and the reality of still having a partner available, even if it's a challenging relationship, seems so different from having to deal with the complete loss of a partner, especially with parenting. I assume they couldn't possibly know what I'm going through as a widow with a young child. I'm coming out of that phase; I understand that even though our stories are different, the suffering endured, the aloneness, and the need to find a new life rhythm may be much the same. I had held on to the thought that I was separate from the world of single mothers, that the death made it all different. But that's not helpful for me. If I isolate and separate myself from the larger world of women who are also raising children alone, whether by divorce, death, or single motherhood, then I miss out on the strength of community and wisdom we all share.

Receiving advice from other single moms leads me to reflect on the conversation I had with a friend who went through a tough divorce when her kids were young. We spoke about the challenge of eating well and how I worried about feeding Lucas a healthy diet. She told me her children ate peanut butter and jelly on soda crackers for several months in the early stages of her divorce. She now has two vibrant and healthy teens that eat kale salad. Enough said. I immediately cut myself slack for the steady diet of quesadillas that are our staple of the last few months. My new focus is to make sure Lucas has access to healthy food. He will survive a few months of quesadillas and veggie burgers.

I've also decided veggie burgers count as vegetables, and if you eat one you can still go to Dairy Queen. But a key point is that it's not appropriate to fall apart emotionally and cry at Dairy Queen (Breathe! Breathe! Breathe!). They don't know how to handle people falling apart, I could just tell. Maybe at the coffee shop, but not DQ. I was tired, and it all felt so sad and alone sitting there with Lucas, eating ice cream as a way to pass the time of a dark fall evening. But it wasn't the place to start crying. There are times to buck up, and this was one of them.

In addition to not crying at Dairy Queen, my new resolve is to actually go to the grocery store. Even if I buy all prepared items from the natural food deli, it's important to have food in the house. The fact is, I'm not cooking, and I most likely will not cook this week.

That cabbage in the fridge will not turn itself into the beautiful Asian slaw I used to make. It will sit for weeks, patiently waiting, but will never turn edible without preparing a nice dressing or wielding a knife to make it smaller. I can turn this around by going to the grocery store and buying pre-made salads and kid-friendly food.

I suppose it's natural to expect that five months after a death, a family would be able to feed itself. But I really wish those amazing meals from friends were still coming. They came for weeks on end, even when we weren't hungry, while Michael was in hospice and then for the month after his death. Stews, soups, salads, and leftovers that lasted days. Now there is a lonely cabbage, apples, and some hummus sitting in the fridge next to the milk. It's time to either ask for help or go to the grocery store.

Tuesday, October 16th

Who knew there would be so many firsts? Since Michael's death, the first time I experience anything I'm caught completely off guard, and the emotions wash over me as if he died yesterday. After nearly five months, the firsts are still surprising me.

Yesterday was the first time Lucas has been sick, and I was completely overwhelmed. He came to me in the middle of the night with a stomachache and then proceeded to throw up all over my bed. I cleaned him up and started the first of many loads of laundry. Then I cried while cuddling him back to sleep. By the time morning rolled around, after two more bouts of vomiting and sheet washing, I was a mess. I projected way out into the future that I will never be able to work, because I will be the only one here to take care of a sick child. I awfulized my way into picturing never being able to do anything for fear of needing to be a parent ready to respond at all times.

In the light of day, I see how negative future-fantasizing is dangerous, very dangerous, and spins me out of the present moment faster than a frog after a fly. Reality is that I'm only ever asked to do what is in front of me. I can do today. I can do this moment. I can clean up vomit and comfort my child, and we will get through this moment. And then the next and then the next. Pretty soon it'll be evening, and we'll watch the new *Stuart Little* movie and

eat soda crackers and drink fizzy water and trust that
tomorrow we will feel better.

Friday, October 19th

Is it weird that I want to bake Michael a cake today? It's his birthday. He's not here to eat it, and I don't need to be eating it. Lucas doesn't know it's his dad's birthday, and I'm not sure I'm ready to deal with him knowing that today. But doesn't it seem even stranger not to bake Michael a cake?

These were the musings I had this morning in wondering how to handle Michael's birthday. I decided not to do anything grand and focus instead on getting through the day. For the last few months, this strategy has served me well for other major holidays. While I made it through nearly the whole day relatively stable emotionally, one moment completely tripped me up.

This moment reminded me of the completely cheesy but lovable 1980's movie *Ice Castles*. In the movie, a young figure skater has an accident at the top of her career, goes blind, is abandoned by the fanciful culture of skating, and returns to the small pond by her rural home where she learns to skate again. She eventually goes back to the national championships and has a perfect skate with no one knowing she's blind. The crowd and all those who had given up on her are awed. The critical moment comes when the fans urge her to circle the ice in celebration. She goes out on the ice, luxuriating in the recovery and redemption of it all, and in response, the fans throw her roses. Unable to see them, she trips, and is reduced to crawling on the ice with the secret of her blindness revealed to the crowd. Her boyfriend, who had anticipated what was needed to keep her secret safe, comes out to help her. As he reaches her on the ice, he says, "The roses, I forgot about the roses."

While not exactly the same situation as a blind skater tripped up in her return debut, it's how I felt today. I got through the day knowing it was Michael's birthday and trying to foresee everything that might catch me off balance. I was steady, strong, met with my grief coach for an hour, took care of my child, and gracefully faced yet another day of pain and emptiness. I did it with confidence, despite going through another first and feeling grief, because I so clearly had a plan of how to meet this day.

And then I went to the mailbox. I picked up the heavy stack of mail and realized the majority of it was cards. Birthday cards. Cards for Michael, who is no longer here. "I forgot about the cards," I muttered under my breath. "I forgot about the cards." Cut at the knees and, like the skater crawling on the ice, I realized again the depth of my loss. There will be no cake, no presents, no cards from anyone that knew him well, and he won't show up for a birthday dinner. He is gone, and while I'm well aware of that fact, I wish the mailbox didn't have to remind me so strongly.

The ironic thing is that one of the cards was from our mortgage consultant, who sends birthday cards each year with a scratch ticket lottery card. I opened the card, figured what the heck, and scratched to reveal the numbers. Won a dollar. Not a million dollars, not the big prize, just a dollar, which seemed fitting for the day. Even if I won a million dollars on that damn scratch ticket, I don't think I would have felt any better. I would have collected the money, put it in the bank, sent some to a few charities, and sat around and wondered if I would ever feel like using that money to make a new life. I already have a blank slate, an opportunity to completely transition to a new life, a new job, a new home, take classes, recreate a career, travel a bit, do anything I want. But there's nothing I want. There is nothing I want other than our life back, before he was sick, before he died, when he came home and we danced and made dinner together. When he would hold me at the small of my back as he kissed me and it would all be well again.

But he's not coming back. Winning the lottery won't change that. Getting a new job won't change that, or moving or travelling to a faraway country in hopes that I will be inspired. So I sit with my blank slate and my grief and I take my steps out on the ice, unable to see, feeling for the edges of the pond, beginning to trust again, and maybe this time remembering the roses.

Saturday, October 20th

It's interesting (although interesting isn't quite the right word) how aware I have become of feeling numb. As the months pass after Michael's death, the shock and numbness are slowly wearing off, and I now notice how raw it feels to be living in the world without the protection they provided.

Four months ago, just a month after Michael's death, I was able to function, but now I see how much I didn't feel. As the anesthetic wears off and I start to feel, it's clear how numb I have been for a very long time. Looking back, it has been well over a year and a half that I've been numb.

Lately, I've been having flashbacks of when we first found out Michael had cancer, and the treatment that proceeded from there. It seems like such a short time ago. He had gone in for a screening colonoscopy with a few mild symptoms of back pain and fatigue that we attributed to a busy work schedule. With him being so healthy, we never imagined the colonoscopy would be anything but a typical quick trip to the clinic. I picked him up that beautiful fall day, with Lucas in tow after kindergarten. I had on a baseball cap and my walking clothes and expected to pick him up at the front door of the clinic and zip home for an afternoon of yard work. I don't know what I would have worn if I had known he had cancer. Something more somber, I suppose, than a ponytail and yoga pants.

I knew something was wrong when he called and said I needed to pick him up inside. It was taking longer than they expected. When I walked into the room, the look on the nurse's face told me everything I needed to know. Someone swept Lucas away, and thankfully he went off easily to play while we took in the news. In a somber tone, the gastroenterologist was already telling Michael they had seen something abnormal. We could hope for the best, but he was almost positive it was cancerous and had already scheduled us with a surgeon.

Is that when I went numb? I do remember standing there with full-tilt panic going on inside, while outwardly I asked what seemed like the right questions. Somehow I didn't fall screaming to the floor. I knew enough about what the doctor was saying to understand we were in for a ride. I remember wanting to cry, but I didn't. I felt like I had to stay calm and take it all in. There should be crying rooms, you know. Rooms in clinics where you can hear terrible news and go cry and scream for a while and then come back and take in all the information. But there wasn't. There was only the racing pace of two doctors and a nurse coordinator giving us the news and then passing out cards, numbers, and appointments to follow up on the next day.

I don't remember much more about that day. I remember holding Michael's hand. He kept saying he was sorry and I kept telling him it was going to be okay. Someone brought Lucas back from the room next door and Michael got dressed. As we made our way from the clinic to the car, a cocoon of numbness began to cloak my life.

I see now that numbness is protective and therapeutic, hailing back to our prehistoric days when one needed a bit of anesthetic after being mauled by a lion. It's a way of protecting a human from making any sudden movements, so as not to bleed to death. Or in our case, it was a way of muting all the information rushing in. Keeping the words at a safer distance, so as not to touch the core of a being ready to shatter.

There are so many flashbacks to the numbness—that time when the welcome cloak covered the feelings so we could function. I felt numb and oddly clinical at his first chemo treatment, where we said a prayer for the chemotherapy to work and then typed away on our computers for the next four hours, chatting occasionally with the nurses.

I felt it back in April, on a flight home from California, when he got confused and I had to nearly carry him off the plane. I knew it was the beginning of the end, but I needed the cloak of numbness so I could get us off the plane and home safely without the reality of his death breathing so close.

I felt it again in a coffee shop where I sat writing when my phone rang. It was the oncologist, who told me, with a catch in his voice, that the cancer had spread to Michael's organs. We needed to schedule an appointment for hospice. Somehow I gathered my things and made my way to the door, and I could have only accomplished that if I didn't feel what was happening.

Many memories have surfaced. But the one that helps me realize how long I've been soldiering on and functioning above my feelings is the one of the day I nearly cut my hand in half slicing an avocado. It didn't seem alarming at the time, and that's what strikes me as most demonstrative of how incredibly numb I must have been for the majority of the time since Michael was diagnosed.

I was cutting an avocado for the tacos I was making. It was probably about seven in the evening, and although I was in a rush, I wanted to make something everyone would eat, especially Michael, who was feeling terrible from the chemotherapy treatments. In my rush, I did what I've told myself I would never do. I used the sharp end of the knife to remove the avocado pit that wouldn't budge. In a flash, the knife slid over the pit, through the avocado, and nearly all the way through my hand. Initially I thought it was just a little cut. But when I put it under water to give it a quick rinse before finishing dinner, I saw my hand laid open all the way to the bones. "Damn!" I didn't panic though, and I actually remember thinking how it seemed strange I wasn't panicking. There I was, making dinner, soldiering on, while my body was in this state of shock and numbness in order to handle the enormity of what had, and perhaps what was about to happen, to my husband.

I drove myself to get stitches that night, and I didn't flinch even when they stuck the needle in to numb my hand. I couldn't feel anything. I just remember the pool of blood below my hand as they sewed it back up. I thought perhaps I was just strong, but now I see, as the anesthetic wears off, that I was in a haze of stress chemicals. A flurry of fight or flight that has lasted for months, and which is just now, nearly five months after his death, wearing off and letting me feel my life again.

The numbness is clearing. I have access to more of the nuances of emotion. For so long, I have been swinging on a pendulum, either not feeling anything or being incapacitated by too much emotion. There has been no middle ground. This was beneficial for functioning, but clearly left me with just a shadow of the normal spectrum of human emotions. And so I begin now to let the feelings back into my experience of life. I let my life in a little at a time, and I feel. I take small doses so as to not be overwhelmed. I cry. I feel joy. I ache. I feel bliss.

I see the emergence of feelings as a sign of healing. As I heal I am feeling again, and I know now to keep the sharp knives and avocados at bay.

Wednesday, October 24th

I have a dear friend who is phenomenally dedicated, for better or worse, to her own liberation. She has committed each day to an hour of meditation and two hours of stream-of-consciousness writing as a way to clear patterns in her life. I spoke with her this evening and she shared with me that after a month of this discipline, she had come to one clear conclusion: "God is not against us."

It seems like it some days; like God is not really on my side. But when I am honest, I too know it's true. God is not against me, even without a month of dedicated writing and meditating. Nor have I been abandoned in a hopeless situation.

So I take this on as a new mantra for today. God is on my side. God is here—or at least what I have come to know as God over my lifetime of spiritual wandering. I see God as being present with me in what feels like a bad deal in a risky card game. God is here with me as Lucas and I create our pirate costumes for Halloween. God is here in the making of soup today, a practice that calmed me and reminded me how both the creation and eating of whole food is a spiritual practice.

God is here in the little things, the little moments, like soup and pirates.

Thursday, October 25th

Every once in a while, I am wise enough to take advice from a dear friend. I spoke to my friend Janet about staying here in Portland for Christmas. I told her how I feel like I need to face the emotion of going through a first Christmas here. Her shocked response was, "Why?" It was one of those responses that had no editing from brain to mouth, so I knew it was her real take on the situation. Her reaction stopped me in my tracks. She then went on to say how I was doing so well facing so much grief, letting it all in, but that the idea of trying to do Christmas at home this first year alone sounded to her like self-flagellation. Point taken.

A half an hour later, I called my sister and told her I was trying to figure out what to do about Christmas. She said, "Well, we all think you should be with us in Denver." And I cried with relief. It was all clear. I saw how much we needed to be with family, how much better it would be for Lucas to be with his cousins, and for me to not be trying to recreate memories that will never be the same. I realized that sometimes in the midst of all this not knowing, there is so much relief in someone just telling me what to do, where to be, how to show up. There is so much to figure out on my own that it makes sense, particularly facing a holiday, to let someone else guide the whole thing. Amen. Done. Thank you.

Friday, October 26th

You would think that, on the day I start my first grief support group, it would be the thing I would have the most to write about. It was indeed interesting and worthy of some writing process. The group setting was compelling and brought forward for me how unfinished I am with the process of grief, and how clearly I need to be a participant, and not the facilitator that I used to be back in my hospice days. I felt heard. I felt like I heard the pain of others and saw the raw reality of the common nature of loss. I cried. I watched others cry as they shared their stories, and I cried my way through my story. I felt like I was in the right place. I was grateful for the courage of the other participants and for my own courage in realizing how much strength it takes to show up in a grief group. There was no hiding; just a clear awareness of wanting to heal. So I am grateful for this group and look forward to the next eight weeks of learning, growing, sharing, laughing, and crying. I hope to learn from the facilitators, so that someday I might again be someone who helps others through this process of loss.

But the real thing I want to talk about is that today I found myself lusting after my hairdresser. Not that this is new to me. He has always been incredibly gorgeous, kind, and funny. A friend recommended him to me this summer, and for the last couple of months, having him cut my hair has been a safe place to be attended to by male energy and to engage in light conversation. He's

magnetic, easygoing, and I have felt safe bantering flir-
tatiously with him—until today. Today, as he was washing my hair, I noticed how it felt to be close to him. I felt
something I would not have told you was present before:
a palpable sweet sensuality that I was both aware of and
awake to at the same time. It felt normal. It felt good. It
felt like I still have a halfway-alive sense of myself as a
sensual being that can feel another person in my space
and be comfortable in how it feels to be close in a completely natural setting.

Today, like any other day I've gone to see him, he told
me I had great eyes. I smiled. I adore him, and he's my
hairdresser, and, in a completely objectifying way that I
don't think he minds, I see him as someone I can safely
flirt with, be close to, talk with, and feel innocent. And
then, as we talked about how hard this year has been for
me, he shared that things were a little bumpy for him as
well, and that he is now in the midst of a divorce. Time
stopped. I think I stopped breathing. Every red alert
alarm inside me went off, and I suddenly was faced with
the actual lustiness I had for this now available man, and
it scared me. Not that I think anything would ever happen, but my fantasy factor went berserk. I imagined him
kissing me, asking me out for a drink, putting his hand
on my back softly as we were seated for dinner. I awoke
inside to my previously diminished sensuality, and it was
simultaneously delicious and terrifying.

Now, I want to be clear here that the chances of us
ever being together or having enough in common to even

have a second date after we've talked all the nuance of yoga and triathlons is incredibly slim. And the more important reality is that I love what he does for my hair and I always want to be his client. This alone is enough to make me never consider overtly flirting with him. But there I was, imagining myself asking him out for a drink or asking if he would kiss me just once so I would know what it felt like to be kissed again. We could have the rebound kiss that gets us through the first kiss after loss. He would be the kiss I could close my eyes in and pretend it was Michael. But he's my hairdresser. He's my hairdresser, and now he's my fantasy kiss. Is it possible that I can live again, be kissed again, and go on dates again? Apparently some part of me thinks so....

Wednesday, October 31st

I've not been writing much lately. Too overwhelmed? No, more like dullness has set in, and I'm trying to find my way out of it into inspiration. Perhaps this is yet another phase, the glum, strange going on yet not going on kind of phase.

I started a couple of support groups this last week. There is the one for me individually, and the new one is a family group for Lucas and I. Both groups are helpful, and yet wildly different. Despite their helpfulness, they overwhelm me perhaps by making the loss too real. I don't feel like writing. I don't feel like doing much of anything. I wake up, get Lucas to school, walk the dog, take care of things at the house, and it all starts over again the next day. The monotony is mind-numbing, and yet when I try to do something more exciting, it feels just the same. Everything feels the same. I can be here paying bills, or out at the grocery store, or playing the guitar, or hiking with a friend, and everything has the same taste of bland. I guess I can call this the bland phase. I don't think Kubler-Ross has that in her stages, but it should be a new one.

I'm in a phase where I don't care who comes or goes, although people who stay for too long make me tired. I don't really care if I'm busy or not, although I get anxious when I'm really busy with a lot of commitments. If I get too busy, I feel as if I'm forgetting something I'm supposed to be doing at home. Yet when I have expansive time here at home, I don't take care of anything. In general, I don't get much done. It's like I'm still aware of the part of me that was present with Michael, and now that he's missing I feel like I'm supposed to be doing something, but the "something to do" part of the equation is gone.

So I try to choose one thing beyond the basics to do each day. One thing a day is my sister's advice, and she made it through a divorce with two kids under the age of three. She tells me that if I do one thing a day I'll make it through.

What's my one thing today? I have the whole day. What's my one thing? Or perhaps I can do two things. I can go to the bank, and I can do some writing this afternoon. I need something to break the cycle of numbing my emotions with snacking in the afternoon. I can grieve *and* eat well. Really, I can. Do I want to? Not really, but I don't want to wake up six months from now thirty pounds heavier. I need something to do, some focus, something to look forward to. I'm a passionate person, and I think I need more interaction with the world even though I don't feel like interacting. I'm a loner who gets lonely. Ok, now I'm just rambling. Do I want to do something with this writing I'm doing? Is this turning into a book? Something tells me to follow the steps, follow my intuition, and follow the resources from this support group. Something very clearly tells me to not let this experience go to waste. Share the journey. I may not think it's important, but it's vitally important to share.

I need to share watching *Spider-Man*, and the power of big energy grief work for kids, and how much Lucas lit up when he went to the support group and was able to be with other kids who have also lost a parent. He's having fun *and* talking about his dad. I can follow this energy. I can follow the contraction and the expansion of how grief works, I can help dispel the myths, I can find the grace and the gratitude without negating the grief. I can share the journey. I won't let this go. I won't let this go to waste, and I won't let the judgment of the outside world in, even if they want to be helpful. I will spend my days writing, and find someone to read it. I can do this.

November

"I am willing to feel the pain in order to remember the love."

Tuesday, November 6th

It's late tonight, and I'm not terribly inspired to write. I got thrown off this morning, and now I'm floundering in the depths of grief. I went to the gynecologist, which on a normal day is enough to throw me off kilter. Although I wasn't enthused to be there, I was doing just fine until the receptionist asked me if I still wanted Michael to be designated for medical information release. I wanted to say, "Well, he's dead, so that won't work anymore." But that wouldn't have come out right. So I said something more tasteful, but she still got flustered. Then I disappeared into somewhere without feeling. I don't think I reappeared until several hours later.

However, I do remember the nurse practitioner who did my exam mention being willing to prescribe me a medication for anxiety and depression, if I wasn't sleeping well. I knew I shouldn't have fessed up to intermittent insomnia but daily medication seemed like a bit of a heavy hand for occasional sleeplessness. I knew she was trying to help, but I could tell she didn't have much experience with grief and would rather prescribe a pill than talk to me about it for any length of time. And then she said it was okay for me to still feel "a little sad." A little sad? Really?

I realized I shouldn't have told anyone that my husband died. I should have gotten through the whole thing without revealing the loss, but that never quite works. It seems to come out sideways in one way or another.

People—particularly health care providers, I'm realizing—freak out around grief and death. It appears to them as something to fix rather than process, and fixing usually means some kind of pill. I tend to think it's perfectly normal to feel "a little sad" about the death of a spouse within six months. And it's going to take more than a sleeping pill for me to feel less than a little sad.

In contrast to the gynecological debacle, it was a relief to be at support group tonight. It felt good to be with people who understand. It felt good to be supported by providers who understand. I understand that the nurse practitioner was trying to be supportive in a way that made sense to her. I'm all for pharmaceutical help if needed, but not in the place of listening. So tonight, it felt good to acknowledge that I'm doing okay. I'm not over the edge. I can sleep most nights, I'm showing up as a parent, I'm getting the paperwork done, my dog is walked, my lawn is mowed, and I bought fresh vegetables today. I'm doing okay.

Thursday, November 8th

It's hard for me to explain the level of exhaustion in my body today after taking time to mourn. In my session with my grief coach, so much emotion came up which I had been holding back on expressing. Afterwards, I was shaky and cold, so I went to bed. I set my alarm for an hour and cried myself to sleep. I woke up to the alarm, set it for another hour, and slept again. All in all, I was in bed for maybe an hour and a half, but it was so liberating to "take to my bed" and let myself not do anything at all other than grieve and sleep.

I did eventually talk to my sister, and took care of a few things around the house. It felt good to be in action, but overall I'm empty and exhausted. I'm not exhausted in a bad way, but in a way where I realize that there may be many days ahead where I need a clear schedule to grieve. I need to be able to trust that there isn't anything pressing to be done, that I can take time during the day to cry, to sleep, to rest, to care for myself, and to not make any commitments to others. I don't want anyone to visit and I don't want to take any phone calls. I need to be alone right now, or at least for today.

In my coaching session this morning, the emotion that struck so deeply was my perception of having completed what one might call my sacred contract with Michael. I saw that I fulfilled for him a place of belonging, a place of unconditional love. Through the manner of his death, there may have been completion in that I loved him no matter what transpired. Resting in bed later, I realized he may not have believed I truly loved him if he had healed, if he had been the spiritual warrior who had made it through and been cured of cancer. I somehow had to love him in all of his humanness; to be completely devoted, no matter what transpired in his illness. And while for me, I would have loved him unconditionally whether through cure or through death, it was perhaps the level of suffering and complete humanness that he had to go through in order to trust that he was completely loved in this world. Perhaps his spiritual lesson was contained within the awareness that he was loved, even in his inability to "fix" this on a physical level.

If his lesson was to believe he was worthy of unconditional love in the midst of pure humanness, what was my part of the equation? It was a clear lesson he helped me to complete in knowing I am safe, I am held, I am loved completely. He helped me to heal the trauma of past relationships, to know that I can be intimately involved and still be in my body. He helped me to feel love, to live love, to know love as a way of being and not something to be done. He helped me be clear with boundaries and to speak up for myself. He taught me to be the love that I am, without attachment to what I do in the world.

The other crucial thing for me to know, and to surrender in remembering how he died, is that I didn't do anything wrong. I didn't create his illness. I know it's irrational, but I carry guilt over thinking I could have done something that would have changed what happened. If only I had noticed earlier that he wasn't feeling well. When he told me his back was hurting, I should have had him visit his doctor sooner. I know I couldn't have known that his back pain was lymphatic metastasis. I know that we were living a busy life, engaged in work, graduate school, and parenting. I knew something wasn't quite right for the few months before he was diagnosed, but neither of us would ever have imagined he had cancer. I can't beat myself up over thinking I should have or could have done something differently. What happened is what happened. He was a healthy, vibrant man who ended up dying from cancer.

As for me, the course of my life right now is to continue to live wholeheartedly. I choose to live, to be here, to not go with Michael so that I can raise our son, so that I can live a life of loving. That life of loving comes to me when I show up for myself, when I have strong boundaries, and when I am the love that is so present within me.

I can ask for what I need. I can take time to be by myself, to grieve, to mourn, to do the work of introspection without feeling like I need to be responsible for anything other than the work of grieving, and the art of raising my child. I am in the shuffle phase of this card game we call life. I ended the last hand in a way that was not in my control. I didn't choose this, and it will take time to shuffle the deck and get my new hand. Then I can lean into things, feel out what might work, and I'll be back in the game. But for now I rest, shuffle my cards, and trust the next deal will be an easier hand.

Saturday, November 10th

Today I am lost and despondent and frazzled and shaky. I'm afraid each day will look like the last two, after I nearly fell apart in grief group. Triggered to the point of instability, I'm now having trouble functioning. In the group, people talked about the way their loved one died. I started reliving the end of Michael's life and was blindsided by the depth of emotion. I remembered in particular the days before Michael died; the amount of pain he was in and how I felt so completely helpless. This morphed into my feelings now of isolation, loneliness, abandonment, and my responsibility to be a good parent when I'm desperately trying to hold it all together. I'm afraid that my ability to feel grateful during the past few months is gone, and this is what real grief is like. Writing a book about moving through grief with gratitude is bullshit. I feel as if I know nothing about the grieving process other than it hurts.

Perhaps knowing that it hurts is the most important thing to share about grieving.

The truth is, I'm angry. I'm impatient with Lucas, and I'm desperately trying to keep us busy to avoid the emotional vacuum that sucks the life out of everything. Everything feels stale and empty tonight and has felt that way all day, but perhaps it's just my perception that life has stalled and tomorrow will be different. I feel like I'm barely holding on. I'm overeating, but at least I'm not drinking, as I know that can be a slippery slope. If television and sugar are the worst of it then I will most likely survive intact. I want to salve this wound, but anything with meaning feels like fire, whereas anything numbing feels good, like a completely appropriate anesthetic.

I want to call off everything. I want to back out of the exciting work I'm being offered for developing communication for healthcare providers. I don't feel qualified or stable enough to create anything. I'm thinking about cancelling Christmas plans so I can stay home and not have to deal with travel, tickets, or even the dog sitter. The simplest commitments seem beyond me. I feel lost and incompetent and afloat in a world going on without me, as I act as if I must go on as well. I am lost.

In the midst of all this, I found a quote on my grief group handout that resonated with me and lifted my spirits:

> *"Hope is the feeling we have that the feeling we have isn't permanent." – Mignon McLaughlin*

And now I'm beginning to believe that all I'm feeling today is an emotion moving through, and tomorrow will be a new day.

Tuesday, November 13th

I miss grabbing a latte with Michael. Which makes me realize why I haven't stopped for a latte in a long time. It makes me miss him. But today, coming out of the grocery store, I needed coffee. So I dropped by our favorite coffee shop and got a short latte and didn't even think of him until I was outside and took the first sip.

This is going to sound weird, but that sip tasted like the memory of him. That single taste brought back a flood of memories from when we first moved to Portland from Alaska. We had a short-term rental on a house and were on the lookout for a new home to buy. We would get up early on the weekends, load Lucas in the car, grab a latte, and drive around all day looking at houses. It was fun, and it was a luxurious treat to have this little routine with him. Just one sip brings it all back.

The difference in this memory is that along with the pain, there is gratitude. I understand now he's still with me in the memories of the things we used to do together. Even the mundane things made me deliriously happy, just to be with him. We were best friends and as happy on a date to the grocery store or house-hunting as we were at a fine restaurant. I miss my friend, and I will be forever grateful for how much joy he brought into the world simply by being in it. I'm willing to feel the pain in order to remember the love.

Wednesday, November 14th

I'm finding I have a newly emerging willingness to expand. I'm ready to expand beyond the basics of simply functioning through grief, which also means being ready to feel everything I need to feel as I open.

I thought it was easy for me to open, to release habits closing me off from feeling anything other than grief. But it's hard to trust that feelings actually do exist beyond the sadness and anger of loss. It's a challenge to feel hope, freedom, attraction, and joy.

In our family grief group, Lucas is becoming attached to one of the male social workers. He chooses him as the one he wants to play with when the kids break out with their facilitators. And now, I notice that he positions the three of us to stand together when we do the closing of the group, as if he's subconsciously trying to connect us. Initially I was okay with it, and found it endearing of Lucas. Then I recognized that I too found myself wondering what it would be like to have someone step in and play a father figure for Lucas, and it touches much too deep of a chord.

I also felt the heat when one of the facilitators of the adult group asked me if I am challenged by Lucas being so incredibly happy and energetic. She wondered if it was hard for me to meet his energy when I wasn't always overwhelmed with joy. Her question helped me to recognize how differently kids and adults grieve, but it touched on my tenderness of how hard it can be to parent a child while grieving. I know this group is healing for us and I'm grateful for all I am learning, but it's not always comfortable to touch on some of the sore spots.

As a means of self-preservation, part of me wants to walk away from all this insightful and supportive help. I want to create space for myself where I'll be safe from the greater depth of emotions already all too present. I know eventually this group will help the grief settle a bit, but I find it challenging and emotionally evocative to be in a setting with so much attention on our loss. Instead of easing the grief, it's bringing it all to the surface at a time when I am slowly starting to feel the nuance of normalcy.

And yet within this family support group, I'm learning about grieving from children. I'm watching Lucas open to grief through play and connection with other kids who have also lost a loved one. I'm learning how to take care of myself so I can support Lucas on his own path of healing. The facilitators talk about the big energy of grief, and how you can help children move through their grief with physical movement and expression. I see this as a metaphor for meeting the world in a way that opens rather than closes. Yet within this lies the assumption that I also am willing to express and move through the emotions that arise as I open. Frankly, I'm too tired for the big energy of grief, whether expressed by me or by my son, but I don't think I have a choice if we want to heal.

Underneath all of this thinking about more openly expressing my grief is an awareness that I didn't cry when Michael died. I realize how traumatized I am by how his death played out. I see now how strong I was for him, and that I held my emotions in check. But all of that is in the past. I can open now. I can let in the full range of emotions without dishonoring his process or death.

Recently, a friend spoke with a minister who we both know and asked him how she could support me through this time of grief. He shared with her that the task before me now is to express my grief as fully as possible, as if I could win an Academy Award for grieving. When that depth of emotion was complete, expansion would come in with no dishonoring of Michael. He said it would be a gift for me if she can be a friend who can support me in such expression.

I was grateful when she passed on this message, and I see that by grieving, I create an opening into expansion. Through the expansion, I have the possibility of a full and graceful life.

I am willing to open, and I see that I already am opening. I want to be blessed and held with gentleness by the world. I want to hold myself and others gently. I want to be seen and held in the expression of my authentic self, both as I grieve, and as I meet the expansion of all that is yet to come beyond the grief.

Wednesday, November 21st

My friend sent me this poem this morning and shattered any belief I had that I was "just fine" facing our first Thanksgiving without Michael. I've been in an avoidance pattern. I know the holiday is coming up, and it will be a powerful reminder of his absence. I want to avoid the emotions. Yet I also know that Thanksgiving is a natural time for people to reach out, as we're in their thoughts and hearts.

From a dear friend in Alaska:

"I woke and as I was making a cup of tea
You came into my mind.

You and your journey.
Lucas and his journey.
You and Lucas's journey.
How deep it is taking you into life.

Have you gotten to
China by now?
And the wisdom
of the East?

If you haven't you will
very soon.
There you will find
freedom...

So will Lucas.

They say we always have it.
I want to believe them.

I am holding you close
and sending you love.
And dedicating my prayers to you and all those in your
orbit of love."

– Laura Stats

I cried hard after I read this poem, because I realize we are indeed still on this journey to freedom— and must first go through the depths. We will get there, to that place of freedom the wise ones assure us exists. I know we will get there, and in many ways we have already found spaciousness in our fragile hearts, as they open once again to the possibility of freedom in our futures.

This poem is such a beautiful reminder of how many people hold us in their prayers, how many hearts have reached out, and how many friends have supported us in the last six months. It's been six months.

We are at the six-month mark, and it's the holidays. On the emotional intensity scale, this sets up a double whammy. Six months feels like a landmark on the grief timeline for me, and for those around me as well. But it seems they carry the expectation that I should feel some relief or a certain level of doing "better." These assumptions, while partially true, are also a heavy weight to bear when coupled with the upcoming holiday season.

I'm irritated with all the questions people have about what we're doing for Thanksgiving. I'm even more irritated by the number of last minute invites we've had for Thanksgiving dinner. I know they're sincere, but in a "Oh God, I hope the grieving widow and her son have a place to go and we should be sure to invite them!" kind of way. I can turn my irritation into gratitude once I can express the irritation. I know there's love between the lines. I can see the love, and I'm grateful my friend Inge had the wisdom and foresight to invite us for Thanksgiving back in September.

This Thanksgiving will be the first without Michael; without his extraordinary cooking and his extraordinarily large heart. He would be the one inviting those grieving, alone, and lost. His table would have room for everyone. We were like that individually, as a couple, and as a family, and I miss his generosity bouncing off my own. He would be so happy today; up early so he could leave work early, and he and I could face the crowds at the store together. He'd rejoice in the chaos and in finding everything he needed amidst the bustle of the day.

Tomorrow, he would have been cooking from the minute he got up. He would also be a little intense in the kitchen for the first few hours until he was sure everything was coming together. He was funny about feeling crowded in the kitchen and had a three-feet-from-the-chef rule when he was really in flow. It threw me off initially in our relationship, and my feelings got hurt when he wanted to cook on his own. But then I learned to relax and watch him thrive in the kitchen. He loved the art of cooking, and I have much more of a sous chef style so we ended up making a good team. Whenever we entertained I would do a little prep and then ask him what else I could do. He would reply by pouring me a glass of wine and telling me to "Take a seat and look pretty" with a half smile that let me knew he was fully aware of irking my feminist nature. But he also knew I would laugh and take the opportunity to sit down for the first time in hours.

Tomorrow it will be different. We will have a lovely afternoon with friends, play card games, and have a nice meal with their family. But it will be a first without him, and I know there will be tears.

I let each "first" bubble up with its own emotions. I honor them deeply and then let them go; making room for the small slice of freedom in my heart that knows he would want me to embrace the newness and spread kindness and gratitude tomorrow. I will miss him this holiday season. I will miss his sparkle, his sense of adventure, his generosity, and his love of celebrating gratitude and generosity. I will miss him.

Saturday, November 24th

"Prayer and love are learned in the hour when prayer becomes impossible and the heart has turned to stone." – Thomas Merton

During a weekend of deep grief on the heels of Thanksgiving, there's not much more to say than this quote.

I am still here.

I am learning to pray, and I am learning to love without the presence of my beloved.

Friday, November 30th

In the process of grasping the reality that Michael is gone, I'm having to step back from grief and toward the present; a present in which he is not here, and yet memories of him are everywhere. I'm not sure how to describe the last month. It's been filled with alternating times in which I'm either completely present to my emerging life, or sideswiped by intense and unanticipated grief attacks.

Yesterday, I was flooded with the acute awareness that Michael is no longer available to comfort me when I'm hurting. I've had a sore tooth the last few days, and yesterday at breakfast I bit down on a nut and a zing of pain went straight through my tooth and into my jaw so intensely that my eyeball ached.

Later, on my walk, I resolved to call the dentist even though I didn't want to believe I needed to go. I was trying to figure out why I was so resistant about going to the dentist when it hit me that I didn't want to face going through a root canal or tooth extraction alone. Underneath the pain, I knew something was wrong with my tooth and I didn't want to have to face it alone. It seemed safer to pretend it never happened and hope it might heal on its own.

I know I can ask for help, but I wanted the comfort of my partner. I can ask for someone to drive me or to look after Lucas, but there will be no one to comfort and hold and reassure me the way Michael did. In longing for comfort, his comfort, I am alone. He isn't going to be here to take over the parenting, tuck me in, make me soup, or blend a smoothie. I will have to coordinate help—a ride, childcare, and my own smoothies. I am alone. I've done this before; I was single for a long time before we met, but having had him, I'm used to a certain kind of loving that feels irreplaceable.

The dental fear triggered a place of feeling alone. So I cried all day. I missed him. I felt like there would never be any way to connect so deeply again and I felt separate from everything that brings me comfort. After the tears, I remembered I have friends who love me, family who will fly across the country for me to have a tooth extracted, and a warm bed to snuggle down into with the memory of my beloved. He is gone, but I am not alone. I am loved. I am connected. I am cared for and I can ask for help. I got to this conclusion not by rationalizing it, but by crying the necessary tears to get me to the other side of this stream of loss.

Other situations will come about where I'll be excruciatingly aware of the aloneness, but this one river of grief has been forded. I can go to the dentist trusting I will pull together the necessary support. I miss Michael's presence, but in this world I am not alone. This awareness, this gratitude for community, is what will pull me through, step by step, tear by tear, into a life full of loving. The blessing of a cracked tooth.

December

"Be gentle, be gentle, I tell myself, and move toward loving. All is well. This feeling will pass, and you will start again tomorrow."

Thursday, December 6th

Today I was able to say out loud that I can acknowledge myself for everything I am doing to heal.

I am healing.

Clarity is coming forward as I step further into choosing to be here, awake and fully engaged. The temptations to be numb, to be a victim, to be lost in grief, are strong. The nuances between feeling and expressing grief, and falling victim to the story of being a young widow, are slippery. As I give my grief voice, as I let the tears come and the anger rise, I allow myself to see, moment-by-moment, how this expression leads to the freedom that waits for me beyond the grief. I feel joy sometimes now. I feel joy when I sing. When I play with Lucas. When I made a Christmas playlist.

The Christmas playlist contained a great metaphor. When I went to burn the playlist, I had to eject the CD already in the computer. Turns out it was a CD with wedding photos on it. I'd found it the day before and spent an hour looking through the photos and crying. And here I was, faced with the metaphor of ejecting that CD and putting a blank one in to burn something new, something refreshing, something uplifting and joyful for the holidays.

The CD has an entire hour of holiday songs. An hour of songs all purchased by Michael and yet pulled together by me. I tangibly brought his memory into the present, and into the future. A future where he cannot be physically present, but in which the ways he lives on in inspiration will be too numerous to count. I am healing. Slowly, surely, integrating the loss and listening to Christmas tunes while I'm at it.

Another yardstick for measuring my healing is experiencing joy and happiness for people in my life who are in love. A dear friend finally said "yes" to getting married to the love of her life, despite her fear of their age difference. Another friend is falling head-over-heels for a man at church, a relationship that I've watched unfold from a front row seat. Rather than being envious or sad, I am truly joyful for them both. I am able to acknowledge the sweet and fleeting nature of true love. What I feel for them is excitement and a sense of urgency. To embrace love fully, to make it their own, and to be in the presence of something that all too easily can disappear.

I may be too aware of the precarious nature of love, but I also have the lived knowledge of love's transformative power. We never know what will happen tomorrow, no matter whether we make logical choices about love or surrender to its force and let it have its way with our lives. The chance of pain is always close, but to be truly known by another human being is well worth the risk. I can't make choices for my friends, but I can revel in watching their love blossom. And I can know what I will choose for myself when love shows up again. I will choose the surrender of love above the logic of reason.

Monday, December 10th

I awoke this morning aware that my focus has shifted away from the general heaviness of grief that for so long has consumed my days. Grief is now moving to the edges of my daily experience, and the lightness of this shift brings much gratitude. Every day still has moments with tears or with the heaviness of grief weighing on my heart, but in general there is a renewed capacity to experience joy and contentment that I thought I might not ever feel again.

My guess is that this shift toward feeling lighter has been slowly happening over time, but I had the experience of tangibly feeling it in family grief group last night. In the adult group, we were discussing how as parents we have the unique opportunity to shape how our children perceive the experience of losing a loved one. The facilitator suggested we consider how we are portraying this experience within the context of our children's lives. This was profound to me. I realized, with distinct relief, that I haven't scripted this experience for Lucas in a way that makes it terrible for him. And now, more consciously, there is an opportunity here in this process of grief to take it further, as a way to help shape the way he sees his entire life. Not that I want to paint a story that isn't true; rather I can adjust the lens.

I would say Lucas is living the experience of grief in an amazingly healthy way, in part because of how intentionally I grieve, and in part because I am giving him room to have his own experience, separate from mine. He's an extremely easygoing and joyful child, and there have been times in these last six months where I've wondered whether he is expressing everything he needs to as he processes his dad's death.

Yet I also see signs of him grieving and accommodating this huge loss. He reacts strongly to disappointment, and a sense of quietness overtakes him when he's overwhelmed. I see him withdraw from his friends, or slam a car door over something that in the past wouldn't have been worth a blink. He expresses that he feels different from other kids, and I notice he has a diminished capacity to recover from schedule changes, or my inevitable refusal of his request for another morsel of sugar at some point in the day. I can reassure myself that he is grieving in a developmentally appropriate way. He craves routine and lets himself feel whatever he is feeling in the moment, without concern for what he "should" be feeling. Even though I don't know exactly what his grief should look like, I can trust he's doing well despite the loss.

Perhaps that is what I want to stress in the "story" of this for both of us. Not that the loss didn't happen or that it isn't and wasn't hard, but that despite the loss, despite believing that this was not the plan, we are doing well. We have a beautiful life with wonderful friends and a tapestry of opportunity before us. We could fall into a story of unrecoverable tragedy, in which we focus only on what has been lost. We could live in the feelings of frustration and anger that this never should have happened. Or we can own the story of picking up the pieces and looking at the future as full of possibility. Our story here is that in the face of the challenge of sadness and loss, we rise. And we do so in a way that courageously and authentically acknowledges our feelings.

This is the story I am choosing for us. A story not about recovery through denial and repression, but a story of recovery that acknowledges the loss down to the very elemental parts of ourselves. In this story, we emerge more whole and with a deeper capacity to meet disappointment, loss, and transition. We can't change what happened, but we can respond to it by learning something that will make us both stronger as we face the inevitable future disappointments of life, both large and small.

Isn't this what I would most want to teach my child, no matter what our circumstances? To meet and grow with every challenge and disappointment that comes his way? To see hardship as part of growth, rather than as a recipe for disaster and doom? I could try to tell him all of this, but the most potent way to share this perspective is to live it, model it, and surround him with people who see us as whole and complete despite the loss. If there's a lesson on resiliency, this has been the graduate level course for him, for me, and even for our friends. I realize that his memories of this time are a reflection of my capacity to meet this grief, this loss, this challenge with grace and courage; to acknowledge the beauty of the life around us as much as we grieve the life that has been lost.

Tuesday, December 18th

Grief should give us a little break when it comes to other challenges, but this last twenty-four hours has shown me that life still happens, and it couldn't be more comedic. It started with Lucas having the stomach flu. In the middle of the night, he came to tell me he felt sick and then threw up in my bed, creating mountains of laundry. Today I found fleas on Alta, which should be impossible, considering she's on flea treatment and our house is clean. A couple of hours later, I looked out the window to see that a giant tree limb from the cedar next door had fallen on our house. Seriously? I can't make this up. I just trust that if things come in threes, I'm done for a while. So where's the gratitude? Miraculously, it's still here, even though I feel like I should have a pass on crazy things like illness, fleas, and falling tree limbs.

I'm grateful despite being concerned about Lucas being sick. It's hard to admit, but I'm grateful Lucas didn't go to school today, as I know there will be conversations about the school shootings in Sandy Hook, Connecticut. I want to protect Lucas from that, and physical illness seems like a fair trade-off for his emotional health. I realize I can't protect him forever, but with all he's been through, he doesn't need to hear about children being shot in their classrooms. And neither do I. Nevertheless, I hold those involved in my thoughts and prayers. I cry, and I protect my child from the impact.

The tree limb didn't do any major damage to the house, and it missed falling from the roof onto our car. I'm grateful it wasn't any worse, and I experienced the support of neighbors who were clearing it from the driveway before I even got it together to go outside.

Which leaves the fleas. I can't yet feel gratitude for the fleas. Maybe more vacuuming will lead me to gratitude, but right now I'm just pissed about the fleas. Seriously. I can do a child throwing up and tree limbs falling, but fleas freak me out. Maybe I'll have an interesting conversation with someone at the pet store when I go searching for a flea remedy. Hope springs eternal, and even a faint sight of hope is cause for celebration and gratitude.

Wednesday, December 19th

Seriously, what is up with the movies about children who are orphans? Last night we started what appeared to be a completely harmless Christmas movie on Netflix. The story started out innocently and then shifted to the plight of a young girl whose parents die and she is sent to an orphanage. The rest of the story chronicles her escape from the orphanage with the help of Santa and his trusty dog. I was stunned, caught off-guard, and more than a little pissed. Why would anyone prey on a child's worst fear at Christmastime?

The plot shift came out of nowhere and hit Lucas like a ton of bricks. One minute we were watching a sweet movie, and then suddenly I'm conversing with him about children in orphanages. I tell him I'm healthy, and that I'm planning on living a long time. And I also acknowledge how this movie might bring up how hard it is that his Dad died. I tell him I'm here for him while I'm trying desperately not to project on him that he's terrified I'll die and he'll live in an orphanage. It reminds me of when Michael was sick. I swear every movie we cued up had in it somewhere that a child's father dies. Couldn't they at least put that in the summary? Aargh!

Thursday, December 20th

The solstice party we attended tonight was a beautiful return to tradition, but it may have been the hardest situation I've been in this last month. The holidays have been challenging, but for the most part I've avoided situations that would have been emotionally evocative. We went to one concert that we always used to go to together, and that was emotional, but otherwise I've found ways around the regular holiday traditions. I've given myself space to simply get through this first Christmas without Michael.

It was with this attitude that I went to the solstice party. It was just an event with new friends; not a tradition I had with Michael that would bring up our story or any requirement to acknowledge the loss and pain. All was well for a while. The overwhelmed hostess was trying to make sushi as guests were arriving, and I took over the task for her. I was grateful to be able to make myself useful and give my hands something to do other than fidget while I made conversation.

I felt confident that evening, even a little joyful at the beautiful community. Organic food, fabulous conversation, kids happily playing, and an awareness that I live in the midst of incredibly talented and lovely people. All was well until we started our solstice ceremony. The kids went upstairs to watch a Christmas movie while the adults dropped into a place of honoring the coming back of the light in the dark of solstice. The offer then came for each of us to share what from this last year we are letting go of, and what we are welcoming as we walk into the light of the coming new year. It was a beautiful process, but damn if it all didn't come up for me. The sudden awareness that there was truly only one thing that happened for me this last year—an unimaginable letting go that was not of my choosing. And how to share that? How to recover from the upwelling of emotion? Or how to simply be in it? To let the discomfort of others not dissuade me from sharing the bald truth that there are no words to describe what has left me this year? How to awaken in the consciousness of the group that there is a loss bigger than they can imagine in their midst?

When it came my turn, I was speechless from the emotion. In that silence, I saw my friend realizing this was not my vision for the ceremony, that there was only one thing that could come forward, and that I was lost in the emotion. My friend came over and held me as I shared my story. I leaned in, opened to her support, and I opened to the space. I shared that the unthinkable had been lost with Michael's death, and I shared the grace that still cradles me: the blessing of a joyful child, the opportunities for gratitude despite the loss, and the awareness of the preciousness of life—the one lost and the ones that go on living. In that one moment I shared what is most important for me, and what I see will guide me as I greet this coming year.

I greet it with the awareness that I have one precious life to live. Not a life that is small and afraid, but one precious life to be lived in complete transparency, authenticity, and alignment. One life. One chance. I have one path to love that honors the return of the light in the midst of darkness.

Friday, December 21st

I spoke with a friend about writing this book and how it feels strange to be saying that I'm writing a book about grief. I didn't plan it this way. I simply wrote about the days as they went by and the words turned into something more, something to share about the process of grief. I started writing to keep my lens focused on gratitude, and in doing so, I have started to write the book on grief I wanted to read but could never find.

I feel shy and awkward about it, considering it's not the most uplifting subject, and it tends to paint a picture of me living in grief. Despite my fears, she commented how it's the perfect time to be writing. How the opening within my consciousness has created a time and perspective on grief that will never be the same. This isn't something I can write retrospectively. This is living in the conscious present during each moment of this journey. I am living grief and sharing from the inside, present moment of the experience. It will end up a healing tool, a memoir, or both, to be shared as a window into my felt sense of what it is like to live through grief.

Saturday, December 22nd

The end of the Mayan Calendar, 12/21/12, passed us by in the night. The day after the world was supposed to end, and I'm still here. The miraculous part is not that I'm still here, but that I'm actually glad to be here. I wondered if it might be easier, with the weight of grief still so heavy, to disappear with the rest of the human race in a Rapture-like event. Part of me wished an outside force would take it all away in one fell swoop. But instead, I am here this morning, and fully glad to be alive. That to me is a sign of healing.

It's sad to think the opportunity of today wouldn't exist if the Mayan calendar had indeed predicted the end. I don't think I had any real belief that it would, especially after someone pointed out that the original calendar didn't count leap years and the world technically should have ended sometime in the 1970's. I'm more grateful to be alive today than I was in my early teen years of the late 1970's. This to me is another subtle marker of growth, of healing, of the awareness that, although I miss Michael deeply, there is still reason to live. Reason that back in June was unclear to me.

Wednesday, December 26th

I suppose it makes sense to mention Christmas and how it was more manageable than most of the days we have walked through in this last seven months. We are at my sister's house in Colorado, and I am incredibly grateful that for me, family is a refuge rather than a struggle. Lucas has been fully engaged with his cousins, and there's plentiful opportunity for me to connect with my sister and mom. I also have the blessing of time to walk in nature and the choice to take care of myself in ways that are difficult at home alone, making my way as a single parent. Perhaps this ease here at Christmastime is a clue for me to consider moving closer to family. Right now my direction is toward stability: keeping the same school, staying in the same house, and being grateful for the incredible amount of support from my friends and community in Portland. There may be a day when it makes sense to move, but for today I am grateful for the ability to travel to family during times when we need extra support. Christmas is one of those times.

I can't imagine having gone through Christmas morning, just Lucas and I. The absence is already so palpable here, with a full house and lots of fun, that to imagine just Lucas and I waking up to the morning, and me trying to make up for all that has been lost through presents, would have been a disaster. Instead, we were surrounded with love, just enough presents for everyone, and the days before and after filled with activities and distraction. Despite my leaning toward feeling the grief, there's much to be said for pure distraction.

Dosing is what they call it in grief group. Opening to the grief in doses is more manageable than letting it all in at once. I see the wisdom here, for how could I open to all the emptiness that comes forward when I think of never having another Christmas with Michael? Or of Lucas never again experiencing the incredible generosity of heart displayed by his father in the spirit of the Christmas season? I couldn't have opened to the fullness of how much that hurts without breaking open into places that would have been unrecoverable in the moment.

I didn't want to spend Christmas Day crying. So I spent only part of the day crying, and the other part I spent enjoying the beauty that every Christmas brings. I let myself be open to the awareness of the day in which the angels hover close to the earth, touching hearts and bringing peace. This was a day to experience healing rather than regret. This year, the spirit of Christmas is embracing the beauty of human angels in the form of family and friends that walk beside me on this journey.

Thursday, December 27th

A subtle change in me acknowledges a strength I've found, that perhaps I never opened to in the past, but have had to acquire in the process of grieving. There's a letting go of acquiescing to others and instead standing forward and taking care of myself. I'm making choices that are self-honoring. Like my choice of going to church when no one else wanted to, and making it happen by asking for what I needed. Or how I didn't have any problem telling friends who live twenty minutes away and wanted us to come for dinner that I didn't want to risk getting caught in the snow. And then the afternoon of Christmas, the emotions began suffocating me. So I went for a walk in the middle of the day, even though it meant stepping out of the activities everyone else was involved in on Christmas Day. I can take care of myself and not have to make it a huge deal to ask for what I need.

I also realize that I don't care what anyone thinks of my choices or decisions as long as I am in alignment with my soul and choosing for my highest good. The depth of loss I have experienced has brought a clarity of intention that simply begs for more authenticity, more embracing of the life I want to live rather than the life other people think I should live. Michael did that for me, he made me strong in standing up for what I want. He believed in me. Now I have the opportunity to believe in myself.

For some reason, I'm even stronger in this capacity than when he was here.

I want to live my one precious life. I want to live in alignment. I want to live on purpose and in clarity. I choose life.

Friday, December 28th

"I do not understand the mystery of grace—only that it meets us where we are, but does not leave us where it found us."

– Anne Lamott

This last week has been one long act of grace. We made it through Christmas, our first Christmas, and I can't even explain it other than an extreme act of grace. For this I am grateful.

Saturday, December 29th

I'm on the plane back home to Portland, and everything is tossed up in the air again. I now seriously wonder if we should move to Denver. It's easier near family. Lucas is in heaven spending time with his cousins and I love the ease of being able to give and receive support from both my mom and sister. Moving would be the easy road. Is there another road, though? Should we stay in our house? Should we stay in Portland? Should I start my own practice or just find a job? What will bring me joy? What is a life fully lived? What are my intentions?

I don't know, but I'm going home to spend some time in retreat. Lucas will come home in a few days with my mom. In the meantime, I'll go to the beach with Alta and walk and write and pray and see what comes clear. I see how I can easily sink into complacency, filling the time with choir, church, volunteering at school, looking for work, and never taking the time to chart a course or direction.

I have set my intention for this gift of time without having to be a parent. My intention is to drop into self-care, to spend time finding direction to create an ideal scene for my future, to sit in the quiet of prayer, and trust that some kind of clarity will emerge. I am living the loving, trusting in Spirit, as I manifest my dreams.

Sunday, December 30th

I can get through most of the day without falling into thinking "this is too hard." I can get through most of the day without falling into despair over everything being changed, nothing ever being as it was before, and how I've lost the love, direction, and calm in my life. Yesterday, or this morning even, I was full of hope, of intention, of believing that I can indeed find a direction for this precious life of mine. This evening I'm watching reruns of *Gray's Anatomy* again and eating chocolate frozen yogurt out of the carton. I'm conscious though, realizing that tomorrow will start anew, and I can choose again to believe in recovery, reconciliation, and reprieve from the grief.

I had grand plans for these few days of freedom from parenting. What I wasn't prepared for was how empty the house would be upon my return. I hadn't realized how much joy and reason for living Lucas gives me. To be here, with the quiet and the time to meditate, do yoga, drive to the coast, take long walks, and write seems like a dream come true for a mother who has been holding it together to have enough energy to parent. Yet I see the other side of the gift of having a young child in the process of grief. I see how he connects me to the necessity of moving forward and choosing to live in joy, lest I mire him in the sadness.

As I sit here this evening, I am aware of a deeper layer of grief that is truly my own, separate from our family and the life Michael and I built together. Being here alone forces me to face the grief of losing him completely. When the house is quiet, there is nothing to stop the awareness of emptiness. When it's just me here alone, I lock the bedroom door when I sleep, out of the fear that comes with the aloneness. When it is just me here alone, I have to make an effort to eat.

I am moving ahead, I am carrying on, and yes, there are still days like today, when I stumble and fall back into the numbness; the salve of anything that will take my mind and attention away. I remember once again that dosing the grief is a natural way to take care of myself.

I didn't do so well with dosing yesterday. I went to the bookstore to get a sense of what other grief memoirs exist in the world. It seemed harmless enough, but how could I think that buying grief books at the bookstore and reading them all evening long wouldn't lead to a relapse? Now I know that it might be better to buy the books one day and read them the next. It's a realistic expectation to not have to do it all at once.

Be gentle, be gentle, I tell myself, and move toward loving. That could just as easily mean watching a funny movie tonight instead of doing more yoga. Be gentle. Be kind. It's okay to lean into joy when you feel sad, to seek distraction from something other than more efforts to find clarity when the grief is too present to see anything clearly. Watch a movie, make some pasta, and get some uninterrupted sleep. All is well. All is well. This feeling will pass, and you will start again tomorrow.

January

"Each small step counts in the thick of the process."

"I realized something I should already know: my husband has died, and he's not coming back."

Tuesday, January 1st, 2013

New Years Day morning. A subtle shift came overnight, and I wake feeling as if the whole world has changed and hope once again resides in my heart. I'm luxuriating in the opportunity to stay in bed and read poetry this morning, and I'm grateful for poems that express the essence of all the possibility I feel on this first day of the new year.

Friday, January 4th

More anger, really? I've been feeling pretty good the last few days; grateful mostly that I haven't caught the flu Lucas brought home from Denver. I've also been feeling confident, competent, and just for the alliteration, a little bit cocky. String a few days of doing pretty well in a row, and a grieving girl gets to feeling like maybe she can take on the world. And so I tried. And what I realized in the trying, without going into all the details of the fabulous career I was about to take by storm, is that I'm still incredibly vulnerable, sad, and angry. I knew the vulnerability was present, but the anger underneath was a surprise, and it came forward with such fury that it shocked me.

I was writing down my feelings, as prescribed by my grief coach, and as I was crying and letting out my sadness, I realized how angry I am that I have to do this all alone. My pen was piercing and fierce. I pointedly inscribed angry word after word about the unfair, horrific nature of losing my husband. I have been betrayed and abandoned. I didn't sign up for this deal alone. I was doing my part, taking care of our home, while we worked toward our dream of building a house and creating our consulting business. I did my part. I held up my end of the deal. I kept things running smoothly; I did the lion's share of the parenting. And now I have to do all that and also find a rewarding career that keeps our finances alive and saves some for college.

And frankly, I'm pissed.

Perhaps more pressingly, I'm not ready. I'm not ready to choose the next great chapter in my career. I worry people will think less of me because I'm not living up to my potential; that I'm not inspired by something. Whatever the something is, it may be smaller than I had hoped. I want to go big, but the rawness of this loss keeps me in a safer arena. In truth, there probably isn't anywhere better for me to be. I wrap my arms around that part of myself that's afraid this is all there is; that's afraid this excruciating grief and fog and boredom around the very fabric of life is all there will ever be. But I'm learning.

I'm learning that, six months ago, I was terrified to travel because the sense of doom was overwhelming. Now I get on a plane and my only worry is whether we'll depart on time. Likewise, this feeling of being left behind in my career—of needing to find something fabulous quickly—is a desire to be somewhere other than in the midst of grief. This feeling will pass and another, less intense one, will come. Slowly, slowly, step by careful step, I will make my way back into the world. I will hope the future holds something different, some inspiration with enough energy to follow through.

Even though I want to figure it all out and make it all better, the truth is I can't right now. My husband died, and I can't make that better. The father of my child died, and I can't change that I'm the single parent of a grieving child. What I can do is listen quietly to my heart. I can listen to the sadness and the vulnerability and the fear, and I can express these emotions in a way that makes sense and perhaps will soothe another aching soul.

For now, it's as though I'm standing on the curb of a busy street and everything is passing me by. The vehicles have a direction and a purpose, and I stand here wishing one of them would be my ride out of all this pain. I know I have choices, and that someday something will feel right; one of those cars will be mine, and I'll drive to something new and bright. For now though, I may as well set up a chair on the curb, take a rest, watch all the possibilities, and trust I'm not being left behind. I'm resting, refueling, and trusting that when the time comes to step forward, I will know.

Wednesday, January 9th

I started out today still feeling the rub of abandonment that's been hanging around for the last few days amidst the shadows and light. I'm angry, and in the wisdom of grief I have opened to the anger. I've written page upon page trying to find the root of the frustration and anger and feelings of abandonment. I'm not angry at Michael so much as I feel cheated out of the years of raising our son together, out of enjoying what we've worked so hard for, out of building our home together. I'm angry that he's gone and I'm left figuring out how to take care of it all. I know I'm not alone in the real sense; that love will always surround me, but in imagining my future, I wouldn't have chosen this picture without him.

While driving this morning, I tortured myself listening to the Jack Johnson live album we both love so much. It makes me miss him, the sweetness of him, so I listened to it in a bittersweet way that was oddly comforting. By the end of the album, I realized why I wanted to remember him today and, more importantly, why I needed to feel him with me. I was afraid. I was headed to the dentist, and I was afraid. I was afraid something wasn't quite right about the planned crown replacement, and I needed him to talk to. I needed for him to walk me through it, or even better, to drive me home so I could take something to relax me before meeting up with a dental drill. I missed his wisdom and his comfort and his steadiness.

In the end he must have been with me, even if just in imagining what he would do and say, because I followed my intuition and told my dentist I needed another x-ray before we did the crown replacement. It turns out we had the wrong tooth as the culprit for all the pain. I ended up getting a filling repaired rather than a crown replaced. Still no picnic, but at least we were on to something that would actually bring relief. I am incredibly grateful for speaking up about my intuition, and for the listening skills and wisdom of my compassionate dentist and her assistant. I still had to be in a dental chair with the drill for two hours, but the sequence of events helped me feel cared for, and in that caring I didn't feel so alone. I didn't get the gentle wisdom and loving of my spouse, but I did get good dental care. Underneath this all was compassion and caring that helped me be less afraid of being completely alone in this life. Damn, this is hard, but I trust I am not alone.

Thursday, January 10th

Having gone through dental work this last week, I notice how stress is taking its toll on my teeth. My guess is that my teeth aren't the only part of my body being impacted, and I wish there was more focus and understanding in the healthcare world on the needs of grieving people. My experience is that grief comes with a whole list of symptoms in the mental, emotional, physical, and spiritual realm. I don't think these symptoms need to be pathologized, but acknowledging them will give people reassurance of their normalcy. Perhaps we could attend a little differently to those who are grieving, and support them in a tangible way that addresses the multifaceted impact that grief has on the body.

I wish every healthcare provider had the skills to acknowledge and understand the symptoms of grief. I truly believe that what doesn't come out in tears will come out in some form in the body, and it's just darn hard to cry enough tears for the body to stay completely whole.

I believe everyone who is grieving needs a good dentist, a naturopath, a physician, a massage therapist, an acupuncturist, and a fantastic health insurance policy that covers it all as basic comfort care.

Tons of studies exist about increased illness and death rates for those who have gone through the death of a spouse or loved one. My calamity of choice seems to be grinding my teeth so hard at night that they break. I remember just shortly after my dad died, I cracked a tooth on a piece of corn bread. Something tells me it wasn't the corn.

I'm sure grief can manifest in the body in multiple ways, including those who are not sleeping well, stressed to the max, dehydrated from crying, and not eating healthily. I believe strongly that we need more health care practitioners who will listen, and are not afraid of grief. Sad to say that first we may need to get them to not be afraid of death.

Friday, January 11th

I have this incredible fear of being left behind, of not being able to keep up, of being unstable and allowing things to fall apart. These fears, nagging at my consciousness, have underpinned some of the emotional outbursts I've had this week. They play into the larger emotion of feeling left behind by Michael, and the reality of how deeply his death has affected me. I haven't wanted to acknowledge it fully, but in the wake of his death, I feel emotionally inconsistent and erratic. I can have a ton of energy and joy running through me one minute, and be in the midst of a crying or angry grief burst in the next. The hard thing is that making decisions from either one of these places is not helpful.

Last week I thought I could take on the world, and had plans to do so. But my plans came crashing down when I viewed them from a place of grief. I so desperately want to be consistent and stable, but going against my natural grieving process will get me nowhere. The stress of trying to keep up—whether literally with my friends and their busy lives, or with my own expectations—doesn't honor my process for finding wholeness.

So I've decided to make my inconsistent and labile emotional state my ally. I can choose to see vulnerability and fatigue as signals that warn me to slow down, take the pressure off, and speak up for my need to take care of myself. Conversely, I can choose to see the moments of energy and drive as harbingers of possibilities to come.

My assumed weakness of emotional instability can now be my barometer for when decisions are ready to be made. For if a decision speaks clearly from both vantage points—from a place of grief and vulnerability as well as a place of high energy—then it truly is the right decision. If doubt lives between the two, then I will wait and trust that clarity is in my future.

I will take baby steps.

All is well.

I can meet my daily needs and those of my amazing son without having to add any pressure for accomplishment. For now, I will focus on integration above ambition, because perhaps integration is the place that truly requires the work now. Anything I could accomplish in my physical world pales to the changing awareness and expansion within as I meet this grief with my eyes wide open.

Saturday, January 12th

I love when people share their stories about the strange ways they've reacted to grief. I just got off the phone with a friend who shared with me that she dyed her hair purple after her father died. She told the story with almost giddy embarrassment, as if just remembering made her uncomfortable. She hadn't thought it was at all funny in the moment, but looking back and being able to tell the story, it became hysterical. The solidarity that came with telling a wild grief story gave her the courage to share it.

We do crazy things when we're grieving. We take long, exhausting road trips, fall apart at the dentist, yell at some guy driving too fast down the street, cut our hair in a fit or grow it out in a long, slow ode to what has been lost. I've been in similar places, and I'm grateful that others who maybe had a drink or two did things that caused them to think the next day about the emotion underneath.

None of these irrational behaviors are without purpose. There is always an emotion waiting to be expressed or a shift in consciousness waiting to appear. But we are not crazy, no matter what it may look like on the outside. Well, we may be crazy, but it's probably the same crazy we were before grief took hold. Grief is an animal moving through our hearts, and the emotions it raises cause us to feel imbalanced and out of sync.

Crazy no. Resembling crazy, yes. Transitory, we can only hope.

Monday, January 14th

Lucas had a beautiful expression today for grief when he said his heart felt droopy. Over the weekend, we were remembering Michael and missing him. We shared sweet memories and felt our droopy hearts.

Tuesday, January 15th

Today, I'm aware that even though I want it to seem so, seven months after a death is not long at all.

Thursday, January 17th

I'm sitting at the car dealer today. This is the first time I've had to interact with the service center that Michael used for his car. I knew I needed to change the service records over to my name, and yet I wasn't sure how to bring it up. So I simply said that I needed to change the service records over to my name, hoping that bypassing any explanation would ward off any questions. Didn't quite work out that way. The service representative asked me if I wanted to keep Michael's name on the account, and I said, "No." She then assumes I don't want anything to do with him, and says something to that nature. She's thinking perhaps we're divorced and I got the fancy SUV in the settlement? Damn. "No," I say. "He died six months ago, and I'm just now getting around to taking care of the car."

Silence. That familiar and awful silence within which we both pause, and then the other person tries to find some way to respond.

I want to save people the pain, but I don't know how. It usually resolves in them saying something like, "I'm sorry for your loss." Followed by downcast eyes and a subdued demeanor. Then I make some light comment to bring us both out of it.

It's exhausting, and I always want to cry. Besides, in certain places it just doesn't feel productive to express my emotions. I've tried every which way to avoid the conversations that lead to crying in places like the car dealership. So today I breathed deeply and focused on the stack of business cards on the desk to keep me from swirling down the rabbit hole of my emotions.

I made it through this "first," and now the car is in my name, and the email reminders for service appointments will come to me, and there is one less place I have to explain the tragedy and respond to people's reactions.

Thursday, January 24th

Last night was a tough one. It wasn't tough in the normal, slow, exhausting march to emotion you can see coming. Instead, it was feeling fabulous one moment then being slapped upside the head and careening into a shaking glob of tears the next.

I had been at choir, where I now feel comfortable going one night a week. Leit has settled back into Portland after his four-month road trip as part of his process assimilating his father's death. He's graciously offering to be with Lucas each week so I can get to choir. It's healing for me to sing; I consistently feel uplifted and positive. As an extra benefit, by the time I get home, Lucas is in bed and I get a night off from bedtime parenting. But last night he was awake when I got home. Leit had done everything he could to get him to go to sleep, but Lucas was completely worked up, convinced he couldn't go to sleep without me. If I had been prepared, I might have been able to shore up my insides and meet this development while still maintaining a sense of peace from my evening. But I wasn't, and so I didn't.

When I went up to help him get to sleep, my first approach was probably not as soft as it should have been. It came out as "It's time to go to sleep," delivered with the tone of "Go to sleep, dammit!" Thank goodness for a little bit of awareness, because when he told me he couldn't sleep, I felt something deeper under his voice and knew he was afraid. When I asked him why he was afraid, he said he was afraid that he wasn't safe. And under that was a litany of fears. The biggest was that he was worried something might happen to me while I was gone. And under that was the emotion that he missed his Daddy, who he said made him feel "safe and secure." I took a deep breath. Settled in. Knew this one was going to be hard.

We talked for a long time. He expressed how much he missed his dad, and how me going away at night made him afraid he wasn't safe. Even with Leit nearby, he still felt his dad was who made him safe. In that tender moment, the whole world of grief through the eyes of my seven-year-old was laid out in front of me. His pain is different from mine, and it's just now emerging. It's as if now, seven months later, he understands that Michael is not coming back. He eventually slept and I eventually cried. I cried so much that I discovered every tissue box in the house is empty. Really?

How can I stay in the moment with him? How can I let him feel and express his pain without projecting that pain into the future? I need to not worry that he will always be afraid. I need to meet this manifestation of his grief in this moment. I can meet this just as I have met my own grief: one breath, one moment at a time. He is going to be okay, just as I am going to be okay, and we will find our way.

Friday, January 25th

I had one of those huge awareness moments today, where I realized once again something I should already know: that my husband has died and he's not coming back. He's not coming back, and I'm living in our house with all his things in place as if he's going to walk in the door and we will resume life as it was before all this happened.

This awareness usually comes to me through a shock to the system. Today it came after talking on the phone to our mortgage consultant. Everyone has been encouraging me to refinance the house. Rates are low, and I hope that refinancing will bring the mortgage down enough for me to stay in the house longer. Even staying in the house for just three more years gives us more stability; a chance for Lucas to finish elementary school and for me to get settled back into working.

I thought I could refinance and everything would be simple and clear. But I forgot one tiny key to refinancing: I actually have to qualify for a loan. Granted, I have a loan, and since I can still pay my mortgage, I can keep the house for now. But the chance of me being able to qualify for a new loan with my current income is impossible. I have no income.

This little detail hit both the mortgage consultant and me at the same time. Then there was silence; the kind of silence that happens only when an unfortunate truth dawns, a clarifying moment in which the dream shatters.

I can't refinance. I'm here in this house, with this mortgage and the accompanying mortgage insurance premium, until I decide to sell the house and move. The windfall of a reduced mortgage is off the table. Damn.

At least the truth brings clarity. I'm grateful for how gentle the mortgage guy was; so soft and knowledgeable. I'm grateful we chose to meet over the phone rather than in person, so he didn't have to witness the good hard cry that came the moment we ended our conversation.

The truth is Michael is not coming back and there are decisions I will have to make about where we will live as well as how to move, what to keep, and what to give away.

Tuesday, January 29th

The husband of a friend of mine is in the hospital, very ill with complications from the flu. I'm supporting her, I'm pulling for him, and underneath it all, I am afraid. I'm afraid she'll see how deeply his illness triggers memories for me. I'm afraid she'll ask me to visit them at the hospital. I'm afraid of being around someone who is sick. I'm still aching from the days, weeks, and months before Michael's death. I can clearly feel the confusion and the sickness, the raw humanness of it all, and I simply don't want to be around illness right now. Fifteen years as a nurse, and the last thing I can imagine doing is being around someone who is sick.

Two weeks ago, just before my friend's husband became ill, I was out to lunch with them. As we talked, I had the urge to grab his hand, to make sure he knew I cared about him. I was drawn to express myself and had this strange feeling he was going to die soon. I remember thinking to myself, "Please don't let it be true." Now he's seriously ill, and I want to understand what's coming through when I feel illness is about to happen to someone. I want to understand the energetics of it all, and I want to know what to do with what I know. For now I will be here for her; a calm voice on the other end of the phone, a place of comfort and of peace that sadly needs to stay miles away in order to be of any help.

Thursday, January 31st

Of all the emotions surrounding grief, anger is the hardest for me. I realized today that I have been keeping myself distracted. Once again, I've not been attending to emotions hidden beneath the surface. I've been working away at volunteer projects, organizing the home office, going through Michael's things, writing quite a bit, and overall staying busy and distracted. I was aware last night, while eating several cookies, that perhaps I was stuffing my emotions. I've been eating "clean" for the last week or so, and then last night the feelings caught up with me and I craved the comfort that sweetness can touch, but never quite fill. I woke up this morning feeling terrible and vowed to discover what is bothering me. Unfortunately, I didn't get to it until after I raised my voice while getting Lucas ready for school, and until after slamming my hand down on the counter hard enough to wonder if I had broken my pinky finger. Not exactly a "mother of the year" kind of morning.

So now I'm working out the anger. I'm learning that having a sick friend has triggered anger and emotions that have gone unexpressed from the last week of Michael's life. I don't like being angry, but I don't like the feeling of anger simmering below the surface even more. I'm looking for ways to let the anger out. I'm writing, crying with a friend on the phone, and going for long walks with steep hills. I need to work all this anger out of my body. Just when I think I'm doing okay, another layer surfaces, and then all that needs to come out. The layers seem endless. I realize how the dosing of emotion this last year has kept me from completely losing it or hurting something, someone, or myself. It's a long haul of release. Unfortunately, the charts in the grief books are right: grief is a process, not an event, and while grief changes over time, it does not simply go away without the outward expression of mourning.

There is a rhythm to letting go of all this grief. I'm flowing in and out, releasing and recovering, and coming back for yet another release. I want it to be over, to be healed. Yet my attention needs to focus on the small steps of accomplishment I make rather than on the overall perception of being "over it" or "healed" in my grief. The truth is, I crumble much less often than I used to, I need to scream alone in my car much less often, and I occasionally feel joy without looking over my shoulder to see if pain is right behind. There is forward movement. Each small step counts in the thick of the process.

February

"I can live my life as a beautiful journey of discovering why I am here, rather than as a sentence to endure as a victim of fate."

Friday, February 1st

So this is where it gets really interesting. Maybe.

I had an experience today that made me wonder what might be available if I open to the possibility of connecting with Michael on another level. I know he's physically gone, yet I'm beginning to believe he may actually be able to be here at times in the spiritual sense; that he can possibly share a message with me or lend comfort when I need to feel his presence in my life.

I don't really know how to explain this. I got a massage today, and as the massage therapist worked with me, she said she could feel Michael's presence. She then asked me if I ever felt his presence or connected with him. It was similar to the question so many other people seem to feel they are entitled to ask me without really knowing how intrusive and painful that question can be. So often when people ask me whether I "feel him," I end up feeling inept, as if I should be able to sense and communicate with Michael, but lack the connection or skill or depth of loving. Or worse yet, they expect me to describe the magical times I really do sense his presence that I don't care to share because it feels so mystical and personal. But today felt different. I could also feel him in that moment, and it caused me to wonder.

Is this possible?

Up until now I was comfortable not knowing whether it was really him I felt when the sun shone through the trees in just the right way, or the CD player got stuck on a song he loved. I accepted it as a deep remembering of him while also leaning into the possibility that he could be gently reaching over from the other side to lift my heart.

Now I want to know if it's really possible.

I need to get my brain out of this and feel my way.

A whole new potential for connecting could be emerging. The interesting thing is that today is the anniversary of the day we first met.

Is he touching in with me on this auspicious day?

Is this possible? Or is it a fantasy played out by myself and the person who feels his presence?

I sat in the car after the massage and wondered if I could feel him. Something....possibly. A tangibility of energy....maybe. I don't know. I just don't know.

Tuesday, February 5th

It was bound to happen. There had to come a point when I had to tell someone who I assumed knew about Michael's death that he had died. I actually can't believe it hadn't happened until now. It completely sucked.

I met my friend Annie at her new office to grab a scarf I'd left there a couple of days ago. She had just run into a preschool mom friend I hadn't seen in a while, and we all hung out for a few minutes, chatting about Annie's amazing new business space. Turns out this friend had recently taken a job as a financial representative for a local firm, and I mentioned it would be nice to come in and talk with her. I assumed she knew about Michael. I should have known.

I should have known by how she asked about work and seemed surprised that I'd left nursing and was focusing on writing. I should have known by the breezy way about her as we set up a meeting for the next week. I assumed everyone within a hundred mile radius knew about Michael. Turns out I was wrong. As we checked our calendars, she mentioned I should bring my guy in. I assumed she meant Lucas, which seemed slightly inappropriate for a financial meeting. She looked at me funny and said, "No, your husband." Without warning, the words tumbled out. "Michael died." No fancy explanation, no cushioning, just the plain clear fact that he died.

Thank God she recovered quickly. She's a no-nonsense gal and was able to switch gears and move into repair mode. But I went numb. I accepted her hug, took her condolences, and was numb. It sounded so cold. "He died." Like I wasn't used to it myself; as if I had just found out as well and had suddenly come to the realization that I needed to take care of the finances, and talking to a financial person made it seem important to express the clear truth of death.

It nailed me, though.

And now I'm home, eating chocolate cookies for lunch, dipping them in milk while the kale and hummus sit in the fridge. I want comfort. I want relief. I want to feed the numbness and make it all go away.

Wednesday, February 13th

A lot of people tell me I'm strong and am holding up really well. It's true that I am holding up well; I am getting through what has been the hardest time of my life. Yet I still cry every single day. I don't need people to see me cry, but part of me thinks that in order to portray myself honestly, I need to admit I cry every single day. Eight months later, and every day still has a point where the feelings catch up and I cry. I think crying makes me stronger, that each tear builds a healthier future.

In the beginning, there were only two things: numbness and crying. Now there's a rhythm in which most of my life feels...well...like life. In between jags of crying, I'm driving to the store, applying for jobs, walking Alta, all in a normal-life kind of way. I even feel joy and spend time laughing and engaging in a life that is incredibly blessed by friends.

Most of my life now feels relatively normal, even to the point where I'm yearning for something new and exciting to come my way. I'm envisioning a new job, a different place to live, and a new expression of creativity. Yet it's this very same yearning for newness that causes me to cry. I had everything I ever needed or wanted in a relationship, and grief rushes in when I reach out to fill the hole that was left.

The grief returns, yet when I look back to the previous months I see I'm spending more time engaging in life. And the hole feels a little bit smaller.

Thursday, February 14th

First Valentine's Day down.

Ouch.

Most of the day was easy. Until I went to what I thought would be a fun way to spend the evening.

Michael and I weren't big on celebrating Valentine's Day, as we were much more into spontaneous adventures, flowers, and date nights. So even though I knew Valentine's might trip me up because of its cultural implications, I didn't worry about it much. A friend invited me to an "Un-Valentine's" party. It seemed the perfect fit, and kids were welcome, so Lucas and I headed off into the evening with expectations of calm and comfort.

What I didn't expect was that an "Un-Valentines" party would be full of singles. So I walked into a singles party with my young son. What I was able to contribute to conversations came out awkward and the very definition of complicated. My friend was so sweet to invite me and introduce me around. I don't think she or I realized I wouldn't know anyone. It felt so strange to be having casual conversation all focused on "What do you do?" and "How did you get to Portland?" I was vague and cautious and terribly aware that Lucas was the only child there. He was bored and jacked up on sugar from Valentine's candy at school. We were an interesting pair.

I made small talk and we left early. When we got home, Lucas played Legos and I stared into space. I was lonely. I felt the years ahead of being a single mom. I couldn't imagine being single or dating or alone. Through the lens of loneliness, all of the options appeared complicated and hard. And then by some miracle, I snapped out of it. I shook the commercialized holiday right out of my bones. I put Lucas in the bath and then into bed. I folded the laundry, poured a glass of wine, and cued up an episode of *Downton Abbey* on Netflix. With a change of perspective, I snapped out of the cultural clutter of Valentine's Day.

I have an extraordinary child, wonderful friends, and a beautiful life full of promise. Today I wasn't ready to talk about who I am or where I come from or what I've been through. Maybe I will tomorrow, or perhaps by next February, or maybe it'll happen without any thought at all. One day I'll be free to be who I am without the story.

Friday, February 15th

I was reflecting on gratitude with my grief coach yesterday. I was reflecting because it finally struck me why I'm writing about gratitude. Gratitude is the golden thread that connects me back to resting in the sacredness of Spirit surrounding death, and to the deep love Michael and I shared as we walked through that experience. He walked me to the other side and let me have a brief look. As the energy of that followed me in the days after his death, what came forward was gratitude.

I could have fallen into victimhood and been completely justified in that. I could have become bitter and sad and unable to engage in the life I had been left in without him. But he showed me something more glorious. He showed me that in choosing to fully see the beauty and grace awaiting us, that I also have the choice to see it here on earth. No matter how much it hurts to be here without him, there is still so much to live for. I chose to live my life as a beautiful journey of figuring out why it is I am still here rather than as a sentence to endure as a victim of fate.

I am here as a message of gratitude. I am here as a message of loving. I am here as a mother, a friend, and a guide for others on this journey. I am here as a writer. I am here to love and be loved, and I choose to stay in a way that is healthy, happy, and grateful. Amidst all the human emotions running in the current of my life, I am grateful to be in the flow. I am grateful to feel the magical golden thread of gratitude that ties me to the ocean of my origins, into which I too will eventually flow.

Thursday, February 21st

Today I had an amazing breakthrough in my grief coaching session. I've been overwhelmed with decisions around finances and IRAs and financial advisors. Today I realized I've been playing into being helpless. I've been looking at my financial decisions from a place of weakness rather than trusting in my ability to learn what I need to go forward. After looking at this through the lens of a giant misunderstanding, I can now stop believing I don't know what to do about finances. I can stop buying in to the belief that I don't deserve to receive financial abundance.

I do not need to be a helpless victim because I am a widow. I have a feeling many widows buy into helplessness around finances if they weren't the ones who managed the money. It's not like Michael was born knowing how to create a retirement account. He learned how to take care of the big picture investments, just as I learned to create a balanced family budget. Now that he's not here, I have the opportunity to learn how to take care of our investments.

This new awareness extends to many areas I have played helpless within since Michael's death. I am not a victim because my husband died. I can be emotionally wrought and grieving and still make wise decisions. I can feel grief and still be a strong woman gracefully picking up the pieces.

I am finding my strength and empowerment, trusting my inner guidance to assist me in learning all I need to know. I can surround myself with wise counsel and educate myself on the basics of making sound financial decisions.

I can feel grief and not be a victim. I can feel grief and cry when I talk about financial decisions and still be able to do the math. My emotions are not a weakness as much as they are a symbol of how much I want to honor the future we were building and creating together. I am learning and growing, and I am receiving financial abundance and wisdom with grace and gratitude.

Thursday, February 28th

I had an appointment down in Lake Oswego this morning. While there, I was flooded with memories of Michael and me looking for a house to buy there. We loved the area, but it also felt it was a little too upscale for our down-to-earth Alaskan lifestyle. I remember checking out a coffee shop in the downtown retail section. We kind of used neighborhood coffee shops as barometers for how friendly a place was. I remembered the local Peet's Coffee and Tea being a friendly place, even if people were a little overdressed for Saturday morning. So today I got a latte there and drank in the memories of our weekend jaunts out exploring neighborhoods.

As I walked out, I caught the scent of flowers by the door that reminded me of Hawaii, and all the expectations of our upcoming trip. I remembered how important that trip had been to Michael. He had a big bucket list, those last few months of his life. Unfortunately, we waited to start ticking items off until he stopped working, and by then it was too late. We knew he only had months to live, but we irrationally thought they would be healthy, vibrant months full of travel and adventures he had always wanted to experience. Turns out we only had two months. Turns out we only did one trip down to California for a school weekend, and I barely got him safely off the plane home.

So the bucket list still pulls at me. The Hawaii trip is booked and paid for, which is a huge financial relief. I promised him I would take Lucas to Hawaii, and I'm glad we have the tickets. Other things are on his list as well. There is the Legoland trip, which I think we can manage. Building a house, which is far off the scale of being doable.

So much on his list was about "us" and doesn't really relate to "me," but how do I unhook from the energy of all the things he wanted to do with us before he died?

How do I provide completion and closure and still enjoy a trip to Hawaii?

How do I live my dreams, informed by our dreams, without giving myself over to dreams that no longer fit without him present?

What's my bucket list?

March

"Tears bridge the gap between grief and life.
Without the bridge life cannot be reached.
So next time you try to stop your tears, remember:
It is your bridge to your evolution."

— Christina Rasmussen

Wednesday, March 6th

There is heaviness to everything today. I fear that my life will never shift from the landscape of grief, that boredom will overtake me and I'll sink into hopeless suburban mom hell without hope of relief or reprieve. Is it possible to think I'll ever date again? Or be fulfilled in a balance of work and parenting? Or make love? Or feel like my future is bright?

We're going to Hawaii in a couple of weeks, and a friend today asked if I was excited. I told her no. She didn't quite understand.

I want to feel excited. I suppose I could muster the emotion. I am looking forward to a change of scenery, but I can't say I'm excited about anything these days. I move from one expectation and event to the next. I figure my way through the finances, the taxes, the parenting, and all the other details. I walk the dog, write some words, love my child, and see a friend here and there. My life is full of beautiful things, and yet it's as if someone has pulled a muted shade between me and my life. I want to feel something, and yet it all seems so far away.

Sunday, March 10th

Some girlfriends and I spent the weekend at the beach. It was such a needed trip. We talked for hours on end, walked the beach all afternoon, danced around the living room drinking margaritas until we fell on the floor laughing, and spent the morning sipping coffee until noon.

I hadn't planned on having so much fun or, more importantly, giving myself the freedom to have so much fun. It was supposed to be two nights, but Lucas melted down every time I talked about going away for the weekend. My mom was here to take care of him, but he was still afraid of something happening to me.

We compromised on me leaving for one night only. I left early Saturday morning with him cautioning me to not get too close to the waves. I worried about him, but I also worried about me needing desperately to get away for a night. I also didn't want to set a precedent of me not ever being able to leave him. I knew he would be fine with my mom, but as I drove to the beach, a heaviness enveloped me. I never expected to be able to lift it in a mere twenty-four hours at the coast with girlfriends.

But girlfriends are magic and have a way of unwinding you quicker than ripping off a bandage. When I finally arrived there were hugs and a few tears, but after five minutes of the tragic story of how hard it was for me to leave home, I caught on that I needed to jump in and enjoy the miracle of the care and nurturing that women can be for one another. It felt so good. Like Girl Scout camp, but with alcohol and coffee.

The other gals all drove home on Sunday morning, which left me with time to take a long walk on the beach by myself before driving back. I walked the shoreline and thought about Michael. At the end of the beach, the waves crashed on the rocks and I realized it wasn't too long ago I would have had a small desire to walk out into the waves, hoping to disappear into the same bright tunnel Michael walked into. So many months I wanted, on some level, to join him, just to ease the pain. But on this bright afternoon I looked at the waves and realized how deeply and clearly I wanted to live. I wanted to be cautious, not just for my son who worried about me getting too close to the ocean, but also for myself. I wanted to live for all that's ahead of me. I took in this amazing awareness, and then I wept.

After walking for a while, I found a spot in the dunes out of the wind and lay down to soak up some warmth from the sunshine breaking through the clouds. As I lay there, the wind against my face reminded me of a poem I had written long ago. In the poem, I asked the wind to help my life companion find me, whether across oceans or mountains. Years later, when I finally met Michael, I gave him that poem as a way to say he was the one. The wind had worked her magic. As I remembered this poem, another one surfaced in my mind:

Lonely again,
but alone never again.
Your breath is beside me as I lie here,
in the dunes by the beach.
The ocean beyond the dunes
reassuringly,
rhythmically,
reminding me of life.

The beach grass crackles ever so faintly
in the wind whispering above my face.
If I walked into the waves in hopes of surrender
I would instead fight for life.
I want to live.
Even without you here, I want to live.

I'm lonely for now,
but alone never again.
There is a parting in the clouds
where beams of sunlight escape through.
Something greater there awaits me,
beyond the waves and water,
less solid than the sands that shift
in a vision of impermanence.
Molded,
shaped,
the dunes ever shifting.

I remember the light that parted for you,

and then the curtain closing off the sun.
It will open for me some day.
But not today.
Today the wind,
and the sand,
and the waves are alive to me.
As I walk on.
Lonely,
but alone never again.

Thursday, March 14th

It's been a heavy couple of weeks, but talking to people about how hard it's been has helped lighten the load. I've been afraid to be vulnerable, and yet the other day I finally opened up to a friend who lives a thousand miles away. I was able to talk with him about the deep loneliness I feel. The strange thing is, that for some reason I really needed to talk to a guy about it. Not just any guy, but a guy I would be very hesitant to be in the same room with because of how desperately I would want him to hold me. I want to be held. I want to be held in conversation, in arms, perhaps even in bed. I want to be held by the strength a guy has, and whether that sounds crazy or not, it worked for me to be held by his words and his voice. We actually talked about sex, and how it's been nearly a year now since I've had any shred of intimacy, and what that's like after having fantastic lovemaking with the love of my life for the previous eight years. It seems unimaginable to start dating, but there was something incredibly liberating about talking about men—and maybe ever-so-slightly thinking about kissing someone again.

And then, lo and behold, I went to choir last night and found myself remembering how handsome that bass in the back row was, and what a great conversation we had last month at our concert.

Oh, boy. I was not ready to feel this.

My body was ready, maybe, but my mind was going absolutely crazy with what it meant to talk to another man. I snuck peeks at him while singing, but at the break he spoke to the lovely new gal in the alto section who is beautiful and always well-dressed and funny and kind, and I found myself a little put off, like somehow I might have dibs on the only single man in the choir. What was I thinking? At least I laughed at myself.

I laughed until I went to put my chair away and he stepped in and took it from me. He said a sweet hello that had me melting and my insides panicking. He continued to talk, we continued to talk, and I wondered if anyone was watching me, like I was doing something wrong and shameful by talking with him. They, however, had no idea what was happening inside of me; the butterflies in my stomach, the racing mind, and my heightened awareness of his sheer maleness.

We drifted into walking out together, immersed in conversation. When I said something amusing, he lightly touched my arm and it rippled through every cell of my body. Out in the dark parking lot, he walked me to my car, and suddenly I felt like I was on a date. Then I really did start to panic. He said he would love to see pictures of my upcoming Hawaii trip when I got back, and I mumbled something about how that would be wonderful. I had the sense that under any normal situation he might have hugged me, but we were in the parking lot after choir, and other people were leaving, and it was dark and I was aware of being a grieving widow. As all this raced through my mind, he extended his hand to shake mine. But it felt like something more, a hand hug if you will. As we pulled away, our fingers hesitated for just a moment. Then I turned to my car. It was impossible to control everything happening inside of me. I was completely turned on. Wow. I imagined what it would have been like to kiss him, imagined what might happen if we met for coffee, imagined crafting an email to him, acting on this desire desperately winding its way through my being. Whoa.

Whoa. Whoa. Whoa. I need to slow down. I don't want to slow down. I want to be held and made love to, and oh, boy, wouldn't that be messy afterwards? It's always the afterwards that gets awkward. I remember this now. Before Michael. The world of dating I thought I would never have to engage in again. I don't want to go through all of that again. I don't want the personal vulnerability of it, the messy afterwards of what happens when I make decisions on biological desires instead of rational awareness of the potential fallout.

I don't want to date again. I don't want to sleep with anyone else. I found my guy. I found the guy that was my guy. I loved everything about him. A few arguments here and there, but for the most part, anything irritating was seen as absolutely lovable for both of us. He couldn't even try to bother me. I had that kind of love. I had the kind of love that was always happy to see each other. The kind of love that I really want to trust I can have again.

Monday, March 25th

I'm on the plane to Hawaii and the whole trip feels surreal. Never before have I headed off on a tropical vacation with such ambivalence. I feel a little bit of excitement, perhaps even some relief at finally taking the trip, but mostly I just want to get through it so I can stop feeling sad about Michael not coming with us.

Just after Michael was diagnosed, while the Stage IV reality was sinking in, we were at a restaurant when he said we should book tickets to Hawaii for that coming weekend. He was thinking last minute, spontaneous and full of life. I was overwhelmed and still in cancer diagnosis shock. He was starting chemotherapy the next week and I couldn't bring myself to think about Hawaii. I see now that we should have gone then, before the treatment, before the symptoms, before his death.

Now our little makeshift family is on the plane thanks to the tickets we bought last year, a mere few weeks before he died. We're on the plane. Leit, Lucas, my mom and I, we're headed to the tropics. I'm unsure and unexcited and yet clear that I need to go. I'm trusting that whatever secrets Hawaii has in store for me will be healing balm for my soul and a window into his. Bless us. Bless this trip, and may we always remember to seize the moment in each and every day.

Wednesday, March 27th

My friend Julie, whose husband also died last spring, lives here on the Big Island of Hawaii. We haven't seen each other this last year, but we've talked on the phone and been of incredible support to one another. Today we met to go snorkeling at one of the Big Island's most beautiful spots, Pu'uhonua O Honaunau, which translates as Place of Refuge.

It was a beautiful day, and with her guidance and gear, I did some of the most stunning snorkeling I've ever experienced. We saw thousands of beautiful fish, sea turtles, and then a magical encounter at the end of the day with a pod of spinner dolphins.

I hadn't expected to be adventurous while I was here. I have to admit that snorkeling is not my favorite ocean activity. I have a fear of fish touching me. I'm not a strong swimmer, and I prefer to have a kayak between myself and the sea creatures living below. But today I stretched, and it felt good to sense adventure in my body.

I followed Julie as she guided me past the first stretch of reef into a second section, which was where we unexpectedly encountered the dolphins. The reef and dolphins were amazing, but the true gift of the day happened on the swim between the reefs. To get to the second part of the reef, we had to swim into deep blue water. I had never swum in the open ocean before, and suddenly had a case of vertigo, feeling as if I would fall to the depths. I turned back and found myself anxiously pulling off my mask and treading water. Fear of drowning infused every cell of my body as I looked back at the quarter mile between me and the shore. I wanted to swim back, but something told me to put my snorkel and mask back on and take a minute to relax in the water. As I reoriented to the water below, the sun broke through the sky and sent scattered light down through the crystal blue beneath. It felt unworldly and intensely beautiful. I felt Michael with me, his breath steadying my own, his support with me as I met this challenge of faith in myself.

I swam on. One moment completely enraptured by the beauty of the light playing through the water below, and another completely sure I was going to be attacked by a shark. I swam that way for what felt like hours, but was only minutes. And then, only a few yards away, emerged a spiral of dolphins, swimming up from the deep toward the surface. The moment was magical, transformational, and unreal.

I swam with the dolphins, and I swam through my fear into the magic of grace. I felt blessed today, by this island and by my friend. We both know grief, and yet today we chose life as that which connects us to this moment and to our futures. Thank you.

April

"We are filling the empty spaces with life."

Saturday, April 6th

I returned from Hawaii to life and routine.

Which means back to the regular Wednesday night choir, which I realize also means the return to the attraction I tucked away in the back of my mind while travelling. Last Wednesday I expected to see his handsome face at choir, but what I didn't expect is that he would come up to talk with me and ask me if I'd like to have coffee sometime. I was flattered, but surprised. I hadn't planned on the feeling of attraction being mutual. It took me a minute, but I recovered, said yes, and then for the next four days alternately freaked out and fantasized until we got together today.

The actual date was surreal. I don't know if it could have felt any other way, but I was surprised by how flat and numb and completely disinterested I was. It's not that I was uninterested in him; it's that I realized who he wasn't. It's not his fault he's not my husband. But for most of the time, I thought how strange it was to be sitting with a man other than Michael, having coffee on a Saturday afternoon. I also thought about how to arrange my life and childcare around, trying to date again. Childcare was never before part of the dating picture, and I was acutely aware of needing to pick up Lucas on time while trying to appear completely present. I never thought about the details.

I talked with a friend about it later this evening. She said maybe fantasizing about being with someone would be more satisfying than a real date until I got more comfortable. Sticking to fantasy would probably be a lot easier on the potential suitors as well.

But I tried today. I leaned in. I said, "Yes." I went on a first date with a man other than my husband and I survived. I even enjoyed being in male company and having him tell me I was attractive. I don't know where it will go from here. Do I want to take it any further? Maybe? Probably not. I don't think I'm ready. I tried though, and that's a huge step.

I'm aware also that, as I think about dating, I have it framed that I'm dating "another" man. Not a man, but another man. As if I have a man somewhere, and yet I'm hanging out with another. Will it always feel that way? Will I always feel married?

Wednesday, April 10th

Well, I wish I could say that the first date led to a second date, which wrapped up my tragic story with a brand new love story and tied a pretty bow on the whole thing. I'd love to portray the made-for-TV movie: the trauma of death, the grief that melds into a new love, the resolution, the happy ending. It didn't quite go that way.

We had a second date after choir rehearsal, and it was sweet. Nothing went poorly; it just didn't go in a direction that felt good or rational or in any way futuristic. The first kiss was wonderful, and then anything after that was way too much. Essentially, it satisfied the curiosity of having a first kiss after being married for years and wondering if I still knew how to have a first kiss with someone new. Turns out I do still know how to kiss, and it's still fun. The only requirement was to not think about Michael while engaged in kissing. And this, sadly, only lasted for a very brief, very soft, and very gentle moment. Being kissed by him initially was like the first time he touched my arm after choir, fleeting and gentle and causing my insides to flutter. Butterflies up and down my neck when he leaned in for that first time and kissed me gently on the lips. And then he kissed me softly on my neck and then my ear. And then came the more urgent kiss leading to more than a kiss. And suddenly I was gone, lost not in the emotions of desire for the man standing before me, his hands entangled in my hair, but instead lost in a wave of loss for what will never be again. Kissing, more than anything else, made me miss Michael.

And then I shut down. I missed my husband. I wanted to be lost in desire, but instead I shut down and missed Michael. I don't know if it was this particular match, or if I'm just not ready.

Afterwards, when I thought about dating again, it brought up anger. I got angry with Michael. I'm angry he's not here to keep me safe and held and loved in this crazy world of dating in my forties with a young child. I'm angry, and I feel more alone than I have in months.

I think I'm hitting deeper layers of what I miss about him. I've missed so many permutations of who he was, but when I bumped up against the edges of intimacy last night, I realized I haven't yet grieved the lover he was to me. I haven't yet admitted he is gone in that realm too. How many other roles will I have to grieve? This one is deep and painful, and I do know it signifies a huge step in healing. Just thinking about dating again, being willing to feel the pain of loss it brings up, lets me know I'm ready for the next layer, the next letting go. I'm ready for the ultimate healing that comes through transformation of grief from what's lost to gratitude for what I had.

Thursday, April 11th

I had a friend ask me today if I could help her on what to say to someone who has struggled with grief for a long time. I wanted to give her this book, but it isn't ready yet. So I gave her the best interpretation of grief I have ever heard, from a professor of mine, Dr. Ron Hulnick. He said that grief in its most simple form is a loss of a place we put our loving. I remember hearing that for the first time and feeling its truth. Now, nearly a year after Michael's death, I know it as true. Moving through grief is about finding renewal in things we love; not as a replacement for what is lost, but as a place to express the love we are and had the blessing to express with them. Michael expanded my heart. I have more love to give now, simply for the space he carved out for me to love within.

Saturday, April 13th

It's been a dark couple of days, very dark. I'm glad to be emerging from that darkness, and I'm grateful for the light. I've been thinking once again about the days before Michael's death. I'm remembering now why I was able to feel grateful so soon afterwards. I was relieved. I was relieved that his suffering was finally over, and mine as well. I've read in grief books how it's important not to feel guilty about feeling relief when the final days of the dying process are over. I remember, as a hospice nurse, talking with families about letting that feeling be part of all the other feelings.

It's okay to feel relief.

As I thought back on those last days and weeks of his life, I let myself remember how hard it was to stay strong, to be clear and loving when every fiber of my being had been stretched beyond its limit. After he died, I could finally sleep for more than a few minutes at a time. I could reconnect with Lucas, and walk out into the sunshine of the day without fear that Michael would die while I was gone. There was so much fear and pain in those last days.

Over the last couple of days, I let myself remember it all. It hurt to remember, to remember my own suffering as well as his. I let it all in and then breathed into the relief. I breathed without guilt and without believing there was anything more to have done. I remember now why I felt grateful afterwards. He was finally at peace, and I could finally rest knowing his suffering was over.

Sunday, April 14th

Today is nearly a year to the day from when we found out Michael's cancer had spread. Just over a month from now will be the anniversary of his death. I'm at the beach, on a mom and kids weekend, with my dear friend Inge. I'm stunned to find I've been enjoying myself nearly all weekend without endless waves of grief taking precedence over the intent to relax and have fun with our children. I am healing. I am recovering. Lucas and I are finding our way back to a consistency of joy that is remarkable.

Monday, April 15th

We had a beautiful weekend at the beach, and then this evening, as I was enjoying the buoyancy of feeling refreshed, Lucas came up the stairs crying. Caught off guard, I asked what happened, thinking he must have hurt himself. He ran to me and said, "I miss Daddy." Boom. We're there again in the enormity of loss. We cry. He tells me how much he misses his dad because he was such a good reader of books at bedtime. I tell him I hear him. He says he wishes he had never gotten cancer. I tell him I wish that too.

I get set for a long conversation and a long cry, but when I turn back, he's singing and putting toothpaste on his toothbrush and getting ready for bed. He's already in the next moment, having moved through the emotion and finding the next moment waiting for him, as children so beautifully do. I bring it up again as he's going to sleep, seizing the opportunity for continued expression, and he talks a bit more. I reassure him he is loved. After he succumbs to sleep, I panic for a moment and think I should be doing more for him. Does he need a counselor? Does he need another grief group? Or perhaps I can keep being present for these fleeting moments of him missing his father. I am present for him as a parent, reassuring him as I reassure myself that grief moves through us and we are still whole.

This perspective of grief reminds me of being on the beach this weekend, standing in the sunshine between episodes of rain as waves break off the shore. I see another squall coming in the distance and equate the pattern with how grief moves in my life. There are times of sunshine, moments on the beach in the sun with its glorious rays beaming with happiness and joy, and then stormy squalls that sweep through without notice. The squall moves through, emptying the beach of people and casting a dark pall across the stretch of beach, but for moments only. It's not the perpetual black of a storm, but a passing blast of intensity that softens with the opening of a cloud break. Beams of light finally, at last, shine through and beckon for grace.

Tuesday, April 16th

Someone bombed the Boston marathon yesterday. All I can think is, "Really?" I'm stunned when something as unthinkable as this happens. As with most news stories, I didn't know about it until a friend told me. I walked to the school bus to pick up Lucas and ran into a neighbor who is originally from Boston. Visibly shaken, she shared the news then started to cry. I will never understand the why of such things, just as I will never understand the why of cancer. Signs, signals, and symptoms of disturbances live in both the body and in society, and yet there are times when the disturbance simply happens, rips through lives and bodies without distinction or care for the fallout.

I stumble every time I hear of trauma, and the grief that follows. After my father died, I was deeply struck by the 9/11 attack on the World Trade Center. I was working as a hiking guide in Alaska at the time, and had been scheduled to be out for the day in the wilderness. I was down at the warehouse with a fellow guide, getting gear ready, when I heard about the twin towers. We turned on the radio, stunned and shocked, and I thought of my dad, whose death was the closest trauma in my memory. None of it made sense. It seemed as if our world was shattered into two, just as in my father's death. One world before the event and one after. A veil that used to protect me was broken. Or more accurately, the illusion of protection was broken.

And now, thirteen years later, having lost my father and my husband to cancer, I'm a little more accepting of life's traumas. When such things happen, I move away from the news and toward community. I no longer believe bad things don't or can't happen. My life has been shattered. Twice. I still believe in the power of love and gratitude and the grace to go on, no matter what. I hope all the runners in Boston do the same and resist that urge to give up, to hide in fear from bombs and death and shattering. In every moment there is the potential for everything to shatter, and there is the potential for grace.

I won't pretend to know the trauma of having a bomb go off in my city. But I do know the trauma of a figurative bomb going off in my life. It stops everything and traps us in an explosion of fear and uncertainty. There are times when I wanted to give up my own life to the event of Michael's illness and death, to succumb to the trauma that changed everything. Just as my neighbor from Boston wondered why she would go to the store and buy healthy organic food when she was just as likely to be killed nonsensically by a bomb in the streets of her own hometown, I too have wondered why I bother to attend to my own health, my own wellness, my own quality of life, when I have lost so much already and something equally traumatic could happen at any moment.

Yes, anything could happen to me tomorrow, and I can use that as a reason to wait quietly for my own death, huddled in my grief, my sorrow, and anger. Or I can see the possibility of something happening to me tomorrow as an invitation to live more fully, more lovingly, more clearly in respect to the preciousness of this one sacred life.

Wednesday, April 17th

I sent some writing to a friend of mine who has recently been diagnosed with breast cancer. She happens to be simultaneously dealing with her mom having advanced throat cancer. We talked one day about how to hold hope within the circumstances of advanced cancer. I told her when Michael was ill, I'd written about my thoughts on hope. Later, she asked if I would send her a copy. When I emailed it, I felt a tug of resistance. I had written about hope before Michael died, how I wanted desperately to have hope for a miracle, and yet I also needed to believe in a hope that everything was okay no matter what happened. I was struggling so much in facing the roller-coaster ride of his illness, and I needed the reassurance of a deeper place of hope that allowed for peace, even in the absence of a cure. I still stand by my writing from those times, when it was so hard to be hopeful. I think it helped me hold hope right up until the last few weeks, when it appeared clear that acceptance of death was the true path to liberation and freedom from suffering.

Seeing as we didn't get what we hoped for, I now have a funny relationship with hope. I'm not sure someone facing a cancer diagnosis wants to read about hope from someone whose path did not end up with the cure we hoped for. I feel tainted. As if a person with cancer might not want to hang out with me for fear that death may weave its way into their story as it did ours.

I have another friend who's dealing with health challenges with her husband. He's got concerning symptoms and is headed for testing to rule out cancer. They're going to the same hospital where Michael was originally treated, and I know some great doctors who can help. But do they want my referral? Do they want a referral from someone whose husband died?

So I'm hesitant with my sharing around people with cancer. Even though I know so much cancer is now treatable, I personally haven't had great experiences with the illness or its treatment. My father died. My husband died. Both were diagnosed with rare cancers at stage four with no previous symptoms. I'm not much for being hopeful for miraculous cures anymore. Two of the most amazing, healthy, and spiritual men I've ever known didn't get a miracle cure. So where's the justice in that? Turns out people sometimes die from cancer, and we can't make sense of it. I can't reckon with it myself, and I sure can't explain it to my seven-year-old son.

But I can hold hope for other people. I can hold hope for miracles and yet also hold the understanding that it's all going to be okay, no matter what happens. To be able to say this from the other side of death seems a miracle. But I suppose that's what hope is, isn't it?

It turned out that my friend with breast cancer loved the writing. She said it inspired and touched her in a way that only someone who has been close to cancer can communicate. I'm glad it helped her, and share it here in the hope it may help someone else.

Holding Hope with Two Hands
January, 2011

I had an image this morning of a way in which I could move back into a place of hope for Michael's healing and maintain balance in my heart. I felt so thrown off when the miracle of the first two months of chemotherapy came crashing down; when he had his second scan and we learned of blood clots, more chemotherapy, and a departure from our original plan to sail through the process of treatment and back into our normal lives.

Turns out we have to find a new normal.

Turns out we have to find a way to hope for a cure and yet be able to roll with whatever comes our way.

Turns out we never know what is coming our way, and we have been given the precious gift of recognizing that in each and every moment.

So now I'm holding hope with two hands. In one hand I hold hope for a miracle and trust that come July he will be done with treatment. We can continue to follow our dream of moving to Bainbridge Island and will be there in time for Lucas to start school in September. I hold one hand full of promise, full of light and love and hope for our future together.

Underneath I have the second hand, the hand holding acceptance for all that is, all that has been, and all that ever will be. An intuitive, knowing hand, that has been through everything and has a perspective much wider than any hope or expectation I can hold in the other more immediate and tangible hand. The second hand is one that accepts miracles and changes of plans and can hold my heart in balance beyond anything I may think needs to happen. This is a hand that holds hope that everything really is already okay.

Wednesday, April 24th

I just used Michael's REI dividend. No story, no crying, no anxiety over whether the cashier might ask questions. I simply said, "My husband isn't going to use his dividend, so can I go ahead and use it?"

"As long as it doesn't get you in trouble at home!" she replied.

I smiled. "No, I'm certain he's not going to use it." A few minutes later I walked out of the store with a little gift from my departed beloved, feeling pretty good about it just being between him and me.

I feel that a lot lately, as if memories are between the two of us. I'm sure people would listen if I wanted them to, but more and more I feel like some of our experiences are a private conversation. Truth is, he would have given me his dividend even when he was alive. As long as I didn't buy anything black. So I bought a cute aqua-colored top and thought of him.

It's not as important to me anymore for the story to be front and center. I didn't need to let the cashier know my husband was dead, or try right then and there to disconnect the account. He is gone, and I will always know that in my heart. But I'm not in so much misery that I desperately need the compassion of the REI cashier.

Oddly enough, this sweet experience comes on the heels of an exceptionally challenging week. I've been checked-out emotionally and in hermit mode, retreating to comfort and cookies. I've been feeling terrible about having gained ten pounds this last year, and have been beating myself up for not being able to get back on track. I'm eating cookies, playing word games on my phone before I go to sleep, and not getting up early enough to do yoga. Self-care is out the window. Yet I wonder if the numbness and the not-doing is another sort of self-care and self-protection.

The thought of this as a self-protection mode came to me after speaking with a friend who produces a spiritually focused radio show. She called me last night, wanting to chat about her upcoming interview on suffering. The minute I heard the word "suffering" I made up my mind not to call her back.

I was tired, and the thought of talking about suffering just made me want to go to bed. But then she called again this morning, and seeing as I was headed to REI, I wasn't quite as closely allied with my own suffering as I was the night before. So I answered the phone.

We had a fantastic conversation about suffering, and more specifically the payoff we get for staying in our own suffering. At the end of the conversation, I realized that although I was stuck in the suffering of emotional eating and shut down, in a larger way I was protecting myself from the pain of overwhelm. I was creating a suffering loop in order to avoid more suffering. What I see now is it doesn't actually avoid the suffering; it avoids the pain, which is uniquely different. To reduce the suffering, I need to let myself feel the pain and understand what's causing it. Sometimes this is such a daunting task that

it's easier to get lost in the suffering rather than identify the pain underneath and find a way to attend to the
cause. However, if I get close to the pain, if I embrace it
rather than run from it, I can begin to ameliorate the
suffering.

So this new flood of pain I was experiencing was triggered when I went out on my edge and opened up to dating again, and the possibility of intimacy. It was a nice
edge to push, but I went too far and felt the intensity
again of all I have lost. I didn't dose it in a small way, and
as a result, became overwhelmed. I found myself in a loop
of wanting to numb out before I can make my way back
to trying again, albeit more slowly and gently. I now
know the root of the pain that was causing me to fall into
suffering. I went on a date and instead of feeling the joy
of a new possibility I felt the pain of loss.

As it turns out, I did have a date today. I had a date
with the memory of my sweet husband. I went shopping
with him at our favorite store and had him buy me something colorful. Something colorful that speaks of spring,
sunshine, and the possibility of new beginnings.

Tuesday, April 30th

So much has happened in the last couple of weeks that it's hard to imagine conveying it all in writing. One of the things I'm noticing is that the energy for writing about grief is slowly fading. In the beginning it was every day, then every few days, then weekly, and now I find my days are filled more with living and less with grieving—and even less in writing about grieving. A natural progress of healing, I suppose.

I have my moments though, nearly every day, in which I miss Michael desperately. Today in the car, I practiced my singing for my upcoming choir concert and had a full-on experience of how much I will miss him being in the audience. He knew how happy it made me to sing, and he supported me unconditionally. When it came time for concerts, I gave that love back to him in song, singing directly to him from my heart. Ironically, the theme for this spring is "Sing to Love, Love to Sing" and is full of love songs. So as I practiced my alto part in the car, I thought of Michael and how much fun it would be to sing about love in four-part harmony to him this May.

I'm missing a lot of things about him this spring. Last weekend I took Lucas to Legoland in California, and although we had a fantastic time, I felt Michael's absence. Unlike me, he loved amusement parks and would prop me up emotionally when I was overwhelmed by the crowds. He would thrive on the chaos and make the whole thing a grand adventure. Without him there, I had to muster the energy myself. I did my best, and we did have a wonderful time. We stayed in the Legoland hotel and did it up right as a way to fulfill a trip that Michael and Lucas had planned to do together last spring. So we closed another loop, fulfilled another promise, and missed him in the process.

The most poignant moment of the trip came when Lucas wanted to ride the "Bionicle Blaster", a ride that has its participants in the wild grip of a factory robot gone wrong, including sharp turns and upside-down moves over a lake. The ride looked terrifying and seemed like a bad idea. Lucas desperately wanted to do it, but wasn't big enough to go alone, and I knew there was no way I was going to do it with him. My friend Susan, who blessedly came along with us, and had taken on the task of riding all the rollercoasters with Lucas, faced her limit on this one as well. Lucas looked woefully over at the ride and said, "My dad would have done this with me." Yes, he would have, I thought to myself. He would have done anything for you, Bionicle Blaster included.

I acknowledged his disappointment, and we talked about missing Michael on this adventure. Luckily, Lucas recovered when I volunteered to go along on the dragon rollercoaster this time around. I guess watching his mom scared silly on a kiddie rollercoaster was almost as much of a thrill as being turned upside down in the grasp of a giant robotic hand. We recovered, and yet there was something important in acknowledging that it would have been different with Michael here.

I see now there will always be times when I will miss him, and Lucas will too. The difference isn't in missing him, but in that we aren't grieving as deeply anymore. We are filling the empty spaces with life; taking the support of helpful friends and creating adventures built for two instead of three. We aren't waiting for him to come back anymore.

It's painful writing that we aren't waiting for him to come back. I know it's true, and yet it's too final to acknowledge in writing. But as the days, weeks, and months go on, we acknowledge it by choosing to live and embrace each day. I know I could have taken the path of not living, of choosing to live in loss rather than in the moment. I am grateful to have chosen to live in the moments available to me, even with the pain. I'm here for something, whether it's to write a book or ride a Legoland rollercoaster, and I want to honor that which is mine to fulfill in this lifetime.

May

"Yesterday I needed to cry. Today I need to dance."

Wednesday, May 1st

I hired someone to do the lawn.

Thursday, May 2nd

It's the time of year again, when the weeds slowly take over the edges of the yard. Last year I didn't notice it because I was up in the bedroom with Michael, watching him breathe, completely unaware of any world outside of the room.

I remember weeding the yard with friends a month later for his memorial service. We weeded the yard and created a beautiful and sacred space, witnessing a miraculous transformation between our tears. I needed something to do that day. I think there's a definition for that expression of grief. It's the busy type that needs a physical task to move the energy through. On that particular day I needed the "keeping busy" manifestation of grief, just as on other days I needed the "take to my bed and cry for the day" type of grief. There are so many theories of grief, most of which hold true for everyone in some way. I now believe, after a year, that we grieve the way we live; each of our own individual personalities and habits shaping the way in which we experience and approach loss. For me, I have learned that movement and being outside is a key element that pulls me out of sadness and toward life.

And just as a year ago I needed to do something physical, I felt that again today and found myself out weeding the yard with two friends visiting from out of town. Normally I'm overwhelmed by the task, but working together, we had the entire perimeter of the backyard finished in less than an hour. As we pulled weeds and talked, I remembered how good it felt last year to be supported in doing something tangible.

The year is circling its way around again. The same flowers that bloomed when Michael was dying last spring are sending their fragrant blossoms into the tenderness of my memory. I'm coming full circle. Sometimes it's painful, and other times I'm grateful that I may be coming to the end of a year's worth of anniversaries, birthdays, and holidays that all had to be experienced for the first time without Michael.

Friday, May 3rd

I was at a neighborhood dinner this evening, chatting outside and enjoying the blessing of adult conversation while the children entertained one another. It started to get cold, and I noticed myself looking around for Michael. It startled me that he wasn't there.

I wanted to lean into him, to have him put his arms around me and feel his steady warmth. But he wasn't there. I sensed the ease between the couples around me, and I felt very alone. Not just because I wanted to be part of a couple, but because I wanted Michael. I wanted his familiarity; the kind of familiarity that comes with years of cultivated loving. I miss him. Just when I was thinking yesterday that I felt pretty steady, I was hit with yet another time of looking for him and feeling the emptiness without his presence.

Saturday, May 4th

When I opened up the mail today, I found a letter from hospice. They informed me that since it's nearly been a year since Michael's death, my formal bereavement support was now complete. It surprised me, and I felt a little abandoned.

I hadn't actually used the bereavement counseling service, so it felt like I'd lost something I'd never had a chance to find. It's a year later, and I'm probably more ready for a support phone call now than I was for the one call I had a couple of weeks after Michael's death. Back then, I wasn't ready to talk to anyone. Now that I'm closer to piecing together a future without Michael, I'd probably get a lot more out of their guidance and support.

But maybe that's not their purpose. Perhaps they're trying to catch those who might fall off the edge. Perhaps I should be grateful they didn't call me more often, and I should take it as evidence of an outward appearance of sanity. Intellectually, I know they're fulfilling a contractual obligation by closing out our file so they have more space for the newly bereaved. I get that I should be well on my way to healing. I also get that I have more questions now than I did last year when everything was too fresh. This only further fuels my inspiration to speak loudly about grief in a society that wants to wrap it up with a bow after a year.

Sunday, May 5th

I still get incredibly irritable when people want to know what I'm going to do with my life—as if that question has ever been appropriate. Why is it that no one before questioned my intention to write part-time and be a mom, but now that I'm widowed they want to know how I'll solve my work, home, and mortgage concerns? They may as well be asking about sex, religion, and politics. It's personal, damn it!

I know they want to help. I know it makes them un-comfortable, seeing me rattle around in this big house and not have a job. But I have plenty to do and I'm not making a mess of my life. I'm actually trying very hard to put it back together, which includes myriad tasks no one can imagine. I'm sure it makes people nervous to know I'm spending my savings in order to save my sanity and spend time with Lucas. Perhaps they think going to a job every day will save my sanity? Right now I can barely dress nicely and get us both out of the house on time a couple of days a week to volunteer at Lucas's school.

This doesn't sound much like gratitude, and today I admit I'm a little on the angry and bitter side. This time last year, Michael was dying, and I believe every cell of my body is acutely aware of that fact. I want this month to be over; the anniversary to be over. Maybe there will be relief at getting through a year, but today I'm not at all sure.

I wish people would ask more about my writing and less about when I'm going to get a job.

I'm angry and bitter and I want my husband back.

I'm grateful that I have the time to chronicle this year. I'm grateful I have the savings to make it possible. I'm grateful I can make changes in my life as I get relief from the intensity of grieving. I'm grateful I can begin to sift through our things as we prepare to downsize.

I'm grateful to be able to write and to know that a good cry and a dose of gratitude will somehow get me through today.

Monday, May 6th

In grief literature, there's a phenomenon called a "grief burst." When I first read about it, I wondered what that meant. But as I experience more and more of them, I understand what they are and why they're called bursts.

I had one this morning.

I came home from a walk and found myself thinking about the yellow poppies I'd seen blooming along the trail. Wham! There it was: a grief burst. One moment I was happily coming in from my walk, and the next I was sobbing at the counter. A few minutes later, I was doing the dishes. It came, it burst, and it left.

I find such bursts stunningly refreshing now that I know they pass through as quickly as they arrive. Before, when I felt grief come in, I was afraid it would be another day under the covers, or a long period of staring off into space, or simply not being able to stop crying. But now that grief comes in smaller, more concentrated packages, I can just let it run through. I see it coming, I make space, I cry, and then I move on to whatever is next. The release seems to be the key. If I don't let the emotions out, or if I'm afraid of what may happen if I start crying, then I end up in bed.

As a hospice nurse, I like to think of it as breakthrough pain. In treating pain, the goal is to have everything relatively stable, with a consistent dose of medication. But for one physiological reason or another, sometimes a little pain breaks through and needs a dose of opioid to quiet the symptoms until the next scheduled pain medication. We call that phenomenon breakthrough pain. Grief feels similar. When it breaks through, I feel the ache in my chest as if it were a broken bone. In this case, tears are my opioid of choice. Chocolate chips are a close second, but they don't always do the trick.

Tuesday, May 7th

I just finished all the estate paperwork with our lawyer. My lawyer, I guess. I cried all the way to her office and all the way home.

Taxes and estate planning are activities that for me are emotionally evocative. The hardest part was remembering the planning efforts Michael and I made near the end of his life. The truth is, we did a terrible job. We tried, but it was just too hard to think about what would happen if Michael died while we were in the process of fighting like hell to hold on to the hope that he might live. And then, when we finally accepted that he was dying, it felt wrong to be talking about planning a life that he would no longer be living.

Estate planning is not an easy discussion. Advanced directives are not an easy discussion. Guardianship of children is not an easy discussion. But I know these are discussions worth having. I now needed to have them again, reframing the documents as a single parent. No one wants to think about death, money, and taxes, but I wish I had thought more about them with Michael. I wish I had something more tangible in place when he died than a retirement beneficiary form. Although I am forever grateful for the planning we did do—for the discussions we did have, for knowing his wishes when it got close to the end—it wasn't enough.

Which is why I find myself so incredibly grateful for the time with my lawyer today. She asked me hard questions about guardianship and money. She asked me questions about how to pass on what is important to me as a parent in the unlikely event I die. She asked me questions about whether I would want to pay for Lucas's college or if I'd rather have him work for part of it to be invested in his own education. She asked if I wanted to pay for his wedding. I cried a little at that, thinking of all the things I might miss in his future. Then I remembered we were only pretending and planning for the unlikely event of my death. No wonder I put this off!

I couldn't believe the insight she had into how to choose guardians and executors and conservators of an estate. She made clear the point that the person who is handed a grieving child may have their hands too full to sell the house. I don't like to think about what might happen to Lucas if I die or am incapacitated, but she made it clear that not thinking about it means I have no say in what happens. Everything could lapse into chaos rather than having a smooth and thoughtful transition.

I did a lot of hard emotional work today, and I'm grateful to have written down my advanced directives. I want my loved ones to know what I want if the time ever comes when I can't make medical decisions for myself. I want everyone around me to do the same so I don't have to wonder while I'm lost in worry about their health.

I'm grateful to have clear directions in my will.

I'm grateful to have had the thoughtful discussion of who will be the best guardian for Lucas and why.

I'm grateful to know that if I die, my retirement will be managed in a way that Lucas won't inherit it all at the tender age of eighteen

I'm grateful to be thinking about putting my values in words as a legacy to Lucas in case I'm not here to teach him.

I'm grateful to be doing all of these things now, while I'm healthy, and while I can think about my death as an abstract event in a faraway future. By doing it now, I don't have to do it at the end of my life. If I ever become ill, I know I will want to focus on life rather than death, so I'm doing it now.

The process included many hard discussions, but they were easier today than they were when Michael was dying. Today I wasn't overwhelmed by late stage cancer, and I wasn't planning against a clock that was running down. I have a plan now. I told my lawyer my wishes and she wrote them down. I now have the freedom to live in the moment, and I trust I have spared the ones I love precious moments in their time of grief.

Today I am healthy and sane and no longer fully lost in the cognitive dissonance of grief and the emotional wreckage of loss. I made plans for the future for Lucas and Leit. A couple hours of my time and a couple of hours of my tears may just save my family months of confusion.

Wednesday, May 8th

I've been melancholic and in tears, without any specific action or memory attached, several times over the past twenty-four hours.

Is it the estate paperwork, or is it that it's May?

I've held my feelings about last year's month of May at bay. I try not to get lost in emotions around wondering why the last month of Michael's life had to be so hard.

I am irritable and fragile.

I also feel more committed to writing than I ever have.

I feel the preciousness and sacredness of this last year. As it draws to a close, I want to be present with each moment as I pass through this first year's cycle of grief.

Life is already taking on its own new rhythms. Leit took a new full-time job, and there's excitement in his energy. My mom is selling her house and moving into a condo to make room for more travel. All around me things are changing, and I also feel the pull toward change and the newness of spring.

Thursday, May 9th

Baseball makes me sad.

Not so much baseball as Little League baseball. Not so much Little League baseball as the apple pie American roots of it all. The dads of the kids who are good players are volunteer coaching. All the other dads show up for games and practices. I think Lucas is the only kid on the team without a dad present.

So, baseball makes me sad. Made more sad by the fact that the "team mom" (how sexist is that?) found out about Michael's death. The other day, she asked me if I'm exhausted being a single parent. I love that she's willing to talk about it, but sometimes I don't know what to say. I guess I could say baseball is not as uplifting as I had hoped it would be.

Not having Michael here for baseball is another layer of grief for what I miss about him. I miss that he's not here to play catch and toss out grounders and pop fly balls. He loved baseball, and he would be so proud of Lucas out there giving it his all, even though he's never even watched a baseball game on television and has no idea about the rules.

I do my best.

I play catch in the yard.

I pitch to him so he can practice batting.

But I'm not Michael. I'm not a dad and I don't watch baseball on TV. I'm not a dad, and baseball for some reason is a dad kind of sport. I try, and I'm actually a pretty good softball player, but that doesn't matter here in the testosterone-filled baseball diamond.

But I'm here for Lucas, even if it makes me sad.

When does soccer season start?

Friday, May 10th

I felt so much sadness yesterday; being a single parent at baseball, driving around listening to Michael's favorite music, being melancholy.

But the waves change, the grief moves through, and today I am happy.

I have energy. When I turn on the car and the melancholy playlist comes up, I realize it doesn't fit for today. So I switch to some dance tracks and groove my way over to the park to meet a friend. Yesterday I needed to cry. Today I need to dance.

Saturday, May 11th

I saw His Holiness the Dalai Lama speak today. I experienced a once-in-a-lifetime event, and it preserves my faith in hope.

Leit's girlfriend, Sarah, was volunteering at the event where he was to speak the next day. She called me the night before to say there was a chance she would have an extra ticket if I wanted to help out by volunteering. I was excited, but as she described the logistics, I suddenly got exhausted and gave up hope we could make it happen. It would have involved getting Lucas out of bed at six-thirty, ready with all of his baseball gear for a ten o'clock game, driving him over to Leit's house on the other side of the city, and then driving down to volunteer at the event until noon, with the hope of a ticket opening up for the afternoon. Just the thought of it exhausted me, and I've learned in this last year to not extend beyond my energetic limits. I politely declined and felt the melancholy seep in, as I wished I had more energy to meet such a great offer.

But as loved ones often do, the three of them rallied to make something happen for me that they knew would touch my heart and raise my spirits. Sarah called me at just after noon to tell me a ticket was waiting. Lucas cooperated beautifully by transitioning quickly from his baseball game to the car, and Leit drove like mad to meet me down at the coliseum just in time to swoop up his little brother. I walked into the talk a few moments later and unbelievably found myself sitting only seven rows back from the Dalai Lama, enraptured and grateful.

The talk by His Holiness was simple in an enduring kind of way, and at end he gave a blessing that spoke straight to my soul. "I am you," he said. "We are the same, you and I. Anything I have done you can do, and it is your job to realize it within yourself." I felt it as a blessing of love and affection, an opportunity to claim compassion as my human birthright. I felt blessed and seen. I was inspired to do the one thing I can do right now through writing: sharing this journey of grief from within. We are all the same, you and I. Compassion and love will see us through.

Sunday, May 12th

This May has been full of times when I sit down and cry. Or stand and cry. Or look at my sweet little boy and cry. Or think of the people who supported us so fully last May and cry. Some of it is sadness. Some of it is loneliness. Much of it is gratitude. The sadness eventually leads to gratitude.

Sitting in the quiet this morning, I thought of a member of the faculty at the university last spring who helped me finish my degree within the circumstances of Michael's illness and eventual death. I had the urge to call her and connect, as clearly as if it was a year ago and she was talking me through another day of caring for Michael. During that time, she was there for us, completely and effortlessly. She knew exactly what to say, and exactly how to be with me—with us—as we walked through the suffering. As I remembered those times of talking to her, when I could barely hold it together, what came forward first was sadness, and then gratitude.

I'm grateful for how incredibly blessed I was to have her participation in Michael's last days, even from a thousand miles away. I truly did feel grateful in the days before and after his death. I had been questioning gratitude, wondering if the sweetness of Spirit surrounding us was an illusion. I started to write gratitude off as being numb or in shock. But looking back and remembering the talks with her, it was real. It was as real back then as it is today, remembering the sad memories of last year, and yet being so grateful for the love that surrounds us.

This time last year was filled with the presence of love. Pure love and a palpable spiritual connection. The energetics of that time are finding me again this May, remembering this month a year ago, remembering the depth of Spirit that wound its way around us in that time when the veil between this world and the next was so thin. I don't know any more now than I did then about what all of it means. But I trust it. I trust it because it is love. Beyond any belief system, beyond any structure, I felt the presence of pure love with us at all times, through the roughest of times. It was real last May, and it's as real today.

This love is as real as the Mother's day poem from my child.

"Dear Mom,
I love you like a butterfly loves nectar,
You are like stars in the night,
as gentle as a ladybug.
I love you."

He reminds me to be grateful for the love that weaves its way in our lives, no matter the circumstances, and to always source from that greater love. With his reminder, how could I not be grateful for the love that is left, even with Michael gone?

We first write love poems to those we love, our parents, our beloveds, until we learn we are truly expressing our love to the source that resides beyond what any person can hold.

Tuesday, May 14th

Lately I've been frustrated with other people's expectations of my grief. Mother's Day is a good example. Friends commented on how hard it must be for me on Mother's Day without Michael. It honestly hadn't occurred to me to be sad about Michael on Mother's Day. Maybe I should have read more into it, and I guess Lucas doesn't have someone making sure he acknowledges the day. But it wasn't a huge trigger for me.

This led to the strange feeling that on Mother's Day I should have been sadder than I actually felt. I suppose I could have mustered up some bittersweet emotions in order to pacify what other people thought I must have been feeling. As if I don't feel grief often enough already?

The same expectation is at play when I hide my emotions; when I'm thrown into grief at something no one else would expect. It's these times when I'm the most alone. Who would think that a particular brand of cracker at a gathering would remind me of him? Or the way the rhododendrons blooming remind me of our first walk in a nearby park? Why is it that I feel like I shouldn't burst into tears when these emotions come flooding through? When I'm alone I do. But when I'm with someone who I think might not understand I swallow my tears. I don't want to deal with their opinion of whether or not I should still be crying over rhododendrons or crackers.

Which brings me to the gift a friend gave me yesterday, when she told me about a woman she met a couple of weeks ago whose husband also died last May. She too has a seven-year-old child. She too endured the long, slow loss of her true love to cancer. She too is wondering if she should sell her house and move to another city. She too has the million other questions of a newly bereaved spouse with a young child. I haven't met her, and yet I already feel less alone in the world of grief. Something about someone else having a similar experience makes my story seem less tragic.

I need times when I don't focus on the tragedy. Perhaps this is what got me riled up about everyone thinking I should be sad on Mother's Day. For once, I wasn't living in the tragedy. I was living in the beauty of my relationship with my son and stepson. I was busy enjoying the blessings of my life.

Over time, my life is becoming relatively normal. It's not always a life in which my husband died, leaving me afloat in a giant sea of grief with a young child to parent on my own.

But at times, all I feel is the tragedy. Knowing that someone else is doing the same, moving in and out of that which has defined us so clearly within grief, makes it all easier. For when my story does arise, I desperately want to talk with someone else who has walked this road.

Wednesday, May 15th

Sitting here writing at our local coffee shop, Maplewood Coffee and Tea, the ambiance and décor make me feel like I'm visiting Nantucket. My neighbor Angela and I write here together each week, inspiring each other to put words on the page. It helps me to be out in the world as a writer. Spasms of self-doubt paralyze me when I write alone at home. The act of being out, writing in the world as the book comes to its final pages, fosters hope and the possibility of what it may become.

Angela and I get down to writing pretty quickly, but we never can resist a bit of chatting over the luxury of a latte with a flower embedded in the foam. Maybe it's because we write together, sharing the intimacy of those first hesitant words on blank pages, that I feel like I can tell her anything. So I talked with her today about how challenging it is to meet new people, people who never knew Michael.

I shared how hard it was at our boys' baseball practice yesterday, walking laps around the field with one of the other moms that I didn't know well. I was on guard about all the questions that are absolutely normal when getting to know someone. "How did you get here? When did you move? How did your little boy get those gorgeous eyes?" The questions that used to be answered in the conceptual container of the family we were when we moved here are now answered from the perspective of a recently widowed single mom. I always do my best to make things vague, and I never specifically mention that I'm on my own now. You would think, with all my talk about our culture not discussing grief, that I would be the first one to wave the flag of open conversation. But I avoid it like the plague because I am afraid of the shock and pity that often follows. I avoid it, but the conversation often comes around to a point blank question that I can't avoid. Something to the tune of, "So what does your husband do for work?" Or, "Is your husband going to the beach with you for the whole week, or just the weekend?"

And here's where I need a little coaching. I tend to say terribly awkward things, like "My husband died." It's a clear and open answer, but still terribly awkward when the other person isn't expecting it.

Angela said to let her know if I ever want her to tell someone first, so I don't have to deal with the startled reaction, even though she probably would sound awkward too, like, "Carole really would love to get to know you, but it's awkward for her to answer all of your questions because her husband just died." Followed by, "And aren't those pretty roses over there?"

We had a good laugh and got back to writing.

Maybe I just needed to laugh about how awkward it was yesterday.

Maybe it's not a big deal.

Maybe I can bear discomfort in order to make the process of death, dying, and grief a little more transparent in the world around me.

I'm writing about it, baring my soul. The least I can do is talk about it at baseball.

Thursday, May 16th

I was exhausted this morning. When I did yoga, it felt like each limb weighed a thousand pounds.

I got home from walking Lucas to school, and the first thought I had was how good it would feel to crack open a beer at eight-thirty in the morning.

I don't usually drink, except for occasionally on a weekend, so this thought actually startled me.

Today hurts.

I feel irritable and angry.

I feel alone.

I feel like no one understands.

I wanted a beer, but I went upstairs and cried instead and stayed in bed for the morning. I slept on and off for a few hours and thought about this time last year, and how much it hurts to think about the last couple of weeks of Michael's life.

I am shaky and my nerves feel shot.

So many people ask me how I am as the anniversary date draws near.

I'm hurting at times, is how I am. And at other times, I do my best to keep moving toward living in the present so I can get to the point where the future makes sense again.

I don't know how to explain it, other than to say I wanted to drink a beer at eight-thirty this morning, and that instead I stayed in bed. After some tears and a couple of naps, I felt like I could make it through the day, and I trust tomorrow will be different.

Friday, May 17th

How is it possible I feel so much better today?

I don't know if I will ever understand grief, but I am blessed to know that heaviness and aloneness do not have to be my constant companions.

Today is brighter.

I'm grateful I talked myself through yesterday with a gentleness of heart that tells me it's okay to hurt, it's okay to go into the pain without being afraid of not coming out the other side. It's okay to trust the weight will lift and lightness will reappear. Over and over again in these tides of emotion, I'm trusting, more than I have at any other time in my life, that there is an essence that never changes and is always present. This essence is unaffected by the rise and fall of emotion. It's unaffected by fears of the future or regrets of the past. It is simply here, the core essence of me, and I am blessed to remember.

Wednesday, May 22nd

A year.

On Monday it will be a year.

It will be the one year anniversary of Michael's death, the one year anniversary of my changed life. It is a year of my life afterwards.

I don't know that I'm different in any externally noticeable way, but I do know that inside I will never be the same. I've been changed by his death and by the grief that has followed. I am more willing to look life in the eye honestly and clearly without fear of reproach. I have faced suffering and sculpted it as much as it has sculpted me. I have lived in the story of suffering, and I have lived in the story of meeting that same suffering with grace.

I no longer want the story to define me as much as I want it to teach me. I want to look back on this year, this time after Michael's death, and see the gifts as well as the grief. But not through denying the grief. At times I have tried to run from grief, but I have never denied its presence, and in that I found my freedom from it. Grief has been a big part of this last year, and I know it will continue to be long after this cliché of the one-year-mark passes next Monday. It has played a large part, but it hasn't defined me as a victim, more as a survivor.

How was I ever able to receive the gift of this awareness so early after his death? Was it the luminosity of the love hovering ever near us in his last days? Or has it been Michael himself, imperceptible and yet here, reminding me to breathe into this life rather than contract into his death? Is it his presence or his memory that calls me to live?

If it isn't his presence, then perhaps it's the steadfast presence of those around me who have come close near the anniversary. Every single person who was here and present this time last year has connected with me this week. Friends call or text daily, checking in as reassurance that the safety net is wide around me. My sister is coming in for the weekend to be with us. Her lighthearted presence will be such a gift. I remember her here the week before Michael died. There wasn't anything anyone could do to make it easier, but she knew to come. She knew she needed to be here, just as she knows to come now. Even though I'm saying I'll be okay this weekend. She knows I need her here.

I'm stunned into gratitude by the amount of support I'm witnessing. It's not just for me, but also for others around me who are also in need. It's as much a gift to be in the role of giving as it is to be receiving. I was reminded of this so clearly yesterday, when my neighbor told me her sister had been in a car accident and was in critical condition. The entire neighborhood mobilized to take care of things so she could drive up to be with her sister. I don't think any of us thought it an inconvenience, and my desire to help was immediate and unconditional. I would do anything she needed. Willingly. In that offer from me to her, I realized the genuineness of all the offers for me this past year, and in the months before Michael's death.

Our tragedy and need for help was not anyone else's inconvenience, but rather an opportunity for a community to rally within a clear purpose of giving. Giving is only possible with the act of receiving present.

So I'm giving and receiving this week. Giving support to a good friend in a very real physical sense by providing childcare and logistics while she is away, and on my end receiving the emotional and spiritual support of so many who are holding us in their thoughts and prayers this week. I breathe in the loving. I breathe out the loving. I breathe in and breathe out, knowing there is only one reason to be here, and there is a very clear reason for why we are not here alone.

Thursday, May 23rd

Grief fog. There's not really a better way to explain it. It's the place where I stare off into space for an awkwardly long time. I go around in circles while trying to get the smallest thing done. I'm out of sync with the rhythm and pace of the rest of the world. Six months ago, I would have judged myself negatively for going numb and checking out, but now I see this process as a protective mechanism from being overwhelmed with grief. I'm taking steps to be more gentle with the anniversary of Michael's death drawing near.

In the fog, I feel stuck. I haven't felt this way for a long time, but I'm being thrown back to a few months ago when this way of being was constant.

I'm irritable, impatient, and want to be left alone with no responsibilities.

I'm flooded with memories of these last two years; both before and after he died, and I realized today how courageous Michael was in facing his death. I remembered his courage and cried and cried over how much suffering he endured. I cried about the physical nature of his suffering in that year and a half before he died, and how for both of us it was also an emotional and spiritual suffering.

This book is about what happened after his death, but there is also a story within what happened before he died. It is the story of who he was and how he met his illness. It is a love story of everything in his life that he wanted so much to continue to love.

Saturday, May 25th

The macabre comedy of death and grief can make me laugh, and that laughter brings welcome relief from the sadness.

My sister and I went through another permutation of sorting through Michael's clothing. Last summer, my mom helped me donate most of his clothes, but many items I wasn't ready to let go of yet. I wanted to be sure that Leit got anything he wanted, and I also wanted to make a box for Lucas so he could remember some of the more tangible things about his father.

Needless to say, many things are still left in his closet, and I am letting them go very slowly.

As my sister and I went through the remaining clothes, I showed her what I was saving for Lucas and got her opinion on what to keep and what to let go of. As we talked, I remembered this amazing dress shirt Michael had. It was a beautiful fabric with fine purple striping that looked stunning on him. He wore it to my graduate school commencement, and it became the go-to shirt for when he wanted to look really sharp.

I was sure I had pulled the shirt out to save, but I couldn't find it. My sister and I both looked for it but without success. And then in the exact same moment, we both realized where it was.

It could have been a very, very, sad moment.

As it was, we looked at each other and burst out laughing.

I had carefully chosen it for the shirt to dress him in after he died. It was his best shirt. We laughed until we cried, and then we laughed again.

Sunday, May 26th

I am in awe and gratitude for the way in which people are showing up to support me near the anniversary of Michael's death. There have been many variations in how they have spoken or acted, but in general what I hear them saying is, "I'm not sure what to say or do to support you, but I want you to know I'm here." The actions have been everything from email, to text, to phone calls, lunch dates, invitations to dinner, and the topper of my amazing sister flying out for the weekend.

I think six months ago, I would have been irritated at all the attention, partly because I wanted to forget how much it hurt, but now I want to be held close by my community, family, and friends at this marker of a year.

I don't know if the day itself will feel any different tomorrow. I do know there is a heightened tension to my days, with the intensity of the cultural expectations around a year of grieving mixed with the memories of all we went through this time last year. The days have had a solemnity to them this last week, as if I'm waiting again for the moment in which he will leave.

Am I waiting for something equally momentous tomorrow?

A throng of angels?

A message from him?

Possibly.

Probably.

I also know the day will pass, like so many others that have gone before without him. But there's something about the anniversary date that makes me think he will be closer. The sort of imagining I do at Christmas, when I think the angels are floating just a little closer to the earth. I can almost hear their faint song between the snowflakes and twinkling lights. There is a similar sacredness to this time of Michael's death, and I suppose there always will be. There will be the memory of the immense light that surrounded our days despite the suffering.

The light will be in the remembering and melancholy of missing him. The story will play out this way, year after year, always a part of the fabric of our lives.

I ask only that tomorrow I am held by the same love that held us for all our years together. I ask that I be held in the grace that got me through the days leading up to his passing, and in the memory of the luminescence of those last moments. I ask that I be held in a way that I can greet the day for whatever it brings. I ask that we be blessed and held not only in our mourning, but also in our living.

Monday, May 27th - One Year

As the circle of this year comes round, the experience of today reflects the year that has passed. I felt grief, yes. And a solemnity that echoed the subdued days of grieving and mourning which passed much of my time this last year. In addition to grief and solemnity, clearly present was an overwhelming gratitude for the web of support and love that surrounds us.

I cried more often today out of gratitude than of grief, whether it was from the texts that came through every hour or so, reminding me that someone was holding us in their heart and prayers, or the knock on the door from a friend bringing a hanging basket of flowers to brighten the deck. The reminders of love and support were numerous and heartfelt.

I felt loved, and I felt clarity in honoring Michael today in a way that symbolized growth into the future that Lucas and I are creating. Leit came over to be with us, and we planted a tree in the back yard, all of us working together to move the soil and create the space. I was concerned about something so permanent being in the yard as a memorial to him, just in case we move one day. But then I decided that instead of feeling that this has to be the only marker of our memory, that we can plant a tree every year. We will plant a tree no matter where we are in the world or what house we are living in, as a way to remember him and the way he encouraged everything in his life to grow.

The rest of the day I spent in the garden, oddly inspired to plant the garden boxes with vegetable starts and put flowers in the planters on the deck. It wasn't something I had planned to do, and up until today, I hadn't had the energy for it. The garden and deck planters seemed like one more thing I didn't have time to take care of this year. But today felt different. Now looking at the sprouts of green tucked into the soil, I can imagine how satisfying it will feel to harvest squash and peas this summer out of the boxes Michael constructed. We created a beautiful space together and whether I sell this house or not, the yard we tended together is taken care of, even in his absence. We continue to sow seeds, to grow, and to anticipate the fall's harvest.

I wonder: what this fall will bring for me? Changes, I know for sure, but towards what end?

I talked to Michael about it this morning in meditation. I often do this, and usually believe it's my consciousness creating a conversation from the memory of so many years together. But this morning was different. I felt as though he was truly present and telling me something, answering something for me that I didn't even know to ask.

I was thinking about the book and this year of grief. I remembered the days before his death and how they culminated in a glimpse of the beauty of that other, less earthly world that lies beyond death. I wondered what it was like for him now, and I envied him residing in a place of remarkable beauty.

Then, without many words but in an almost palpable sense, I knew he was trying to communicate all that was possible on the other side. I heard him say, "Here, you can do anything and everything is possible." He smiled, and then said, "And the amazing thing is, you can too!" It was as if he was saying, "You can do anything there on earth, but you simply don't know it."

It took me a minute to assimilate what he was saying. Then I felt him take my head in his hands and kiss my forehead, as he had done so many of our days together when he was comforting me, or helping me to understand something important. And then he was gone.

"You can do anything too, you simply don't know it."

Everything is possible.

Everything.

Even learning to live again.

Even learning to sing again.

Learning, one note at a time, to sing once again.

A Few Final Notes on Grief

"As long as we sing, the pain of the world cannot claim our lives."
                                                              - Mark Nepo

March 1, 2015

This book could have ended on any day, as so many of the entries followed the ebb and flow of living with grief. I could have continued writing, adding another two years of what it has been like to live in the process of letting go of grief and opening up to life. It turns out though, that the day I was inspired to start writing, the day after Michael's death, was Memorial Day, and the one year anniversary also fell on Memorial Day. It seems fitting to have it end there, on a day dedicated to remembering.

After Michael's death, and in the early months of grief, I wasn't able to see many of the gifts and lessons that were filtering their way onto the pages. I simply wrote each day to find my way through it. I couldn't see anything consistent because everything was always shifting. It was only later, during the process of transforming my journal into a more readable manuscript that I began to see the rhythms and lessons that appeared in the time after his death. In a strange way, writing about grief has given me a new depth of expression. The strength, grit, and grace I had to call forward in response to his illness and death were a greater force than I have ever encountered in my life, and the willingness to tell this story has freed me to live from a more authentic place.

If there is one overarching theme to this story, it is that his death created a place of strength in me, an unbreakable place, a place greater than the suffering itself. Before Michael died, I had wondered if I possessed this place, but I had never experienced it. His death reinforced the wholeness in me that carries through all circumstances. It is the breath beside the breath, containing the essence of all things beyond this world. I believe it is a place of wholeness available to us all.

Would I give this wisdom up to have him back? Yes.

Does it mean I believe he had to die so I could find this place of strength? No.

I don't know why he died, and I may never truly understand. I know his death changed me. But I believe the essence of him resides in that beautiful light he showed me just before he left this world. The same light will meet me some day on the other side of my own doorway into the beyond. I hope I will know then what it all meant.

For now, I choose life, and I choose it knowing I am accompanied by a love and strength that is always with me as I live out my own path. I believe that same love is accessible to all of us who are learning to live amidst the losses of life.

My hope is that some part of my story has inspired you to move more fully into life, whether to embrace a loss or to open to the awareness of how precious our lives are in each moment. These notes are not a step-by-step guide for healing grief, but rather are my sharing of the repeating themes I believe are important, particularly as they have stayed with me over the last two years of continued healing.

I offer these final notes on grief as highlights from my own road map; a map that was roughly drawn while travelling the road of grief. I know each journey is an individual one, and yet in talking with others who have experienced loss, I know the commonalities run deep. It is my hope that these notes offer a sense of validation and comfort for anyone walking a similar road. I also hope they offer insight for companioning those who are grieving or suffering from loss. Watching those we love suffer, whether through illness or grief, is an excruciating experience. We can all benefit from acknowledgement of the losses that run through our lives because grief exists in so many places, even without an accompanying death. In speaking the truth of grief, we are gifted with a grace that will see us through.

The Altitude of Gratitude

Gratitude was the ticket for me to finding a way out of grief. It gave me altitude in the times when I needed to pull up and out of a downward spiral. It didn't circumvent or bypass the grief—I think that would have been false gratitude—but it helped me see the beauty in small things. Over time, gratitude became the largest part of the landscape because it helped me see the things that made life worth living.

Gratitude moved me from one grace-filled view to the next until the tenuous path that held me to life became stronger with the beauty and color of what lay before me.

The little things I could find each day, even the smallest ray of light in the darkness, helped me to live in gratitude.

I invite you to look for what brings you alive. A poem, a flower, the cool water in your throat as you replenish the liquid lost in tears. There is always something. It could be as close as your breath moving in and out or the heat in your home on a cool day. Maybe you'll find it in the scuffed shoes that take you on the walk out the door as you satisfy your dog's need for exercise. The same shoes that surprise you by bringing you to the cherry tree whose blossoms await you as a sign of spring, or to marvel at the first flakes of snow on a winter's day. Perhaps you will find those shoes stepping into the crunchy orange leaves of fall, or supporting you within the sweet whisper of a warm summer wind.

In every season there are delights waiting for you to notice them. If you open your eyes, you will see that the world is still here, waiting.

The Shifting Tides of Grief

I began to write early on after Michael's death because writing has always soothed me and helped me to find normalcy in the most challenging times. As I wrote down my experience, I often wondered if grief would take over and I would lose my mind. Grief was foreign, unstable,

and unlike anything I had ever felt before. My whole being was affected—mental, emotional, physical, spiritual,
and mystical. But then I started to see the rhythms, the
repeating themes, and the shifts within that went from
despair in one moment to manic joy in another. Patterns
of waves appeared. Eventually the image of grief as waves
moving in and out within the tides of remembering
helped me become more stable. Imagining grief and the
need to mourn as a wave that rises and falls in the ocean
helped me trust the experience would pass.

The waves of grief, when given room to flow, eventually led to calm seas. I held tight to the times when I did
feel stable and made those moments my life rafts. I invite
you to notice the waves. If the waves aren't constantly
engulfing you, if your head can remain above water long
enough for you to catch your breath, then you can trust
you are not drowning, you are only grieving, and this
wave will pass. And if the waves are too much and the
seas are too stormy, it is wise to call for a rescue. I invite
you in these times to call a friend who can be present for
you or a professional who can support you as you make
your way through the waves. I invite you to know that
you don't ever have to be alone in grief.

Surviving Awkward Moments, Finding a Tribe, and the Fine Art of Receiving

I used to think the profession of hospice nursing was the ultimate small talk stopper. People would ask me what I did and my reply, "I'm a hospice nurse" would be followed by an awkward silence. Inevitably, I soon found myself looking for someone new to talk to. At times I left out the hospice part and just went with "nursing," but I found the people I most wanted to talk with were the ones who were comfortable with awkward moments or were thrilled to talk about death and impermanence, even in social settings.

I've found the same with friends who have supported me when my life was consumed with illness or grief. The ones who are comfortable with the possibility that I might cry are the ones who have stuck around. They are the ones I'm willing to talk to and be open with in a place of vulnerability. They are the ones who don't get the traditional "I'm doing okay" or "I'm fine" when they ask how I am. They understand the erratic, mixed-up jumble of emotions that come with creating a new life after loss.

These friends are the primary colors on the new landscape of my life. They are my family and my longtime friends, and while I don't want them to have the shared experience of losing their husband, I'm grateful for their willingness to lean in and try to understand. Critically important in this picture are the other young widows

I have found who do understand what it's like to lose their life partner. I can share things with them that I don't want anyone else to ever have to know and experience.

That doesn't mean there aren't other shades of friendship. In the grief group I went to early on, we were asked to make a list of the different kinds of support we needed, and to match the people in our lives with that type of support. It was a stunning new thought for me that not everyone had to let me cry on their shoulder. I could be supported by people who had no idea of what to say or do, but truly wanted to help. I did the blessed exercise of accepting that there were people who would be willing to drive me to the airport as long as I was willing to talk about the weather instead of Michael. They wanted to do something and the best way to support them in supporting me was to accept that a deep grief conversation was not going to happen and didn't always need to happen. When I needed something more emotionally substantive, I could call someone who was willing to go a little deeper.

The beauty of this approach is that eventually I was able to go out to a movie or an art museum and not talk at all about grief, not even have it come up. It turned out there was a whole cadre of people that fit into the category of being able to completely distract me from grieving when I needed it most.

Underneath it all, people want connection and they want to help. The largest barrier to me receiving that help was twofold: my own inexperience with receiving help, and the expectation that support needs to look a certain way.

In retrospect, I wish I had made a list of all the support I needed. People kept telling me to make a list, that it would be easier for them to help. They were right. A list is like a permission slip for receiving. No matter who you are—grieving or not grieving—chances are you need help with something. We all do.

I invite you to make a list. Write your permission slip, ask for what you need, and let go of your attachment to how it should look. I guarantee that most of the time people will give more than you ever imagined asking for, because by asking, you make the gift of giving possible.

Floundering in Firsts

In the beginning, shortly after Michael died, I was awash in firsts. There were the day-to-day kind of firsts: a trip to the grocery store, the urgent care with a feverish child, a dinner party, a camping trip. All those firsts were shockingly impactful. It was as if the empty space where he should have been reverberated, like the aftershock of an earthquake. Those firsts made it all too real that Michael was gone.

Later came the bigger, more momentous firsts. I could see those coming. The birthdays, holidays, and anniversaries all shook me in that first year. While these were challenging, they were easier to prepare for, and like remembering to stand in a doorway during an earthquake, I could brace myself for the impact. The only thing I wish I had known was that it was perfectly fine to just get through the first round of these more momentous firsts, especially the holidays. I always felt I should be doing something more poignant or honoring of him on those days. But honestly, looking back I can see mere survival was plenty.

I have more perspective now and I can decide more thoughtfully if I want to create something to honor the days when we wish Michael were with us. There are still big days to come, a steady stream of firsts that will coincide with life's major events. I will miss him being there. I will wonder what advice he would give us on such occasions. And I will do my best to bring his memory alive so we can imagine what he might feel, do, or say.

I invite you to imagine with me what someone in your own life might say if they're not present. Perhaps write them a letter and craft a response you can envision them writing back to you. And I also invite you to be gentle; to know there is no right or perfect way to memorialize someone other than to let the memory of them open into your heart and lead you to whatever feels right.

Awash in Feelings

I never knew I could feel so much. I admit I'd spent a decent portion of my life avoiding expressing my feelings. Grief cured me of that. I found the best way to release grief was to move toward my feelings and release them through the outward expression of mourning. Initially this didn't make sense, but as I tried it, as I leaned into feeling more rather than less, I found that the more I felt the more quickly I shifted towards balance.

This process of moving toward grief rather than avoiding it reminds me of swimming in the ocean and having to get past the wave break before reaching the calm water. If I fight the waves as they tumble pass, I inevitably get knocked over. But if I dive into them, head straight into the thickest part of the wave, I emerge beyond it and can ready myself for the next wave without sand in my suit and salt water up my nose.

Similarly, diving deeply into the waves of grief let me see underneath the chaos of the churning foam. Feeling the waves rather than fighting them eventually moved me to more peace and calm. I could see the feelings pointing toward what I needed: to cry, to lie down, to talk to someone, to take a walk. Left churning in the fight to keep my emotions down, I couldn't see anything but pain.

When I had the courage to dive down into my emotions, what I often found was that I was lonely, overwhelmed, or afraid. Once I knew what I was actually feeling—once I moved beyond the chaos—I could act to ease the pain.

It's hard to move straight toward grief when our instincts tell us to pull away, but I invite you to lean in, just a little, feel a small dose and see what your heart is asking for underneath the crest of the wave.

Shock, Numbness, and Autopilot

I remember being surprised at how numb I felt after Michael died. I felt like I should be feeling more, but was unable to access my emotions. Little did I know, the ferocity of the grief when it did arrive would more than make up for the times of numbness where I functioned on autopilot.

The muting and the dulling of emotions are there to protect us from the impact of the truth. Shock is a survival response, and allows for functioning when the body and psyche would otherwise be awash with chaos. When I look back, I'm grateful for the soothing anesthetic that flowed in and out of the early days of grief. It got me through the details of cremation, memorial services, and paperwork. It muted my emotions so that my foggy mind could function on what little energy was available. It held me safely back until there was room to wail. It let me play with Lucas and comfort him instead of being consumed by the ocean of my own grief.

In the end, whether I was numb, wailing, or somewhere in between, I came to realize that whatever I was feeling was the right way to be feeling. I could let go of worrying about whether I was feeling too little or too much. I could release the need to figure out what grieving should look or feel like in any given moment. I figured out there are no rules to grieving or mourning and I could be free to be present with whatever felt most authentic in the moment.

I invite you to be gentle with yourself in your perception of grief.

I invite you to find a place where judgments are set aside and comfort, self-care, and acceptance lead you to wherever your heart, mind, and body need to be in your process of grieving.

Shifting the Lens to Love

I remember Michael telling me about a realization he had on a busy sidewalk one day. He said he looked around at all the people and saw that "Everyone was doing the best they could in each moment to move toward greater loving." He noted several people in his line of sight who were impatient or pushing, but underneath it all, he sensed a drive toward loving. I believed him. I often feel love is just below the surface. But I was also a little cynical because it was hard to believe when I saw people acting unkind. He qualified it by saying that some people just have better aim than others. That was a little easier to take in, and it's a phrase I go back to when I'm challenged in interactions with others who may not be gentle or understanding with the experience of grief.

People often say things to those who are grieving without any idea of their impact: like voicing their woefully inaccurate expectations of the length of time appropriate for grieving; making invitations to dinner parties where only couples will be present; complaining about how hard it is to have a spouse out of town for a week; or asking questions about whether I'm done missing Michael and ready to be dating again without realizing those are two different topics with mutually exclusive answers.

I can choose to be frustrated by all these unintentional slipups and misconceptions. I can choose to take it all personally and rail against insensitivity at a time when I'm feeling raw and vulnerable.

Or I can choose to adjust the lens to loving.

One choice leads to more isolation, the other to connection. I've chosen both routes these last three years and what I've found is that isolation and frustration are challenging additions to a plate already full of grief. In contrast, the path of forgiveness and gentleness greets the energy of support.

A lens of loving helps me accept that people are trying their best. When I choose to see the effort, then I can see the love between the lines. I can be authentic, explain why something is painful, and be direct about what would be more supportive. I can also choose to see the gift of them reaching out at a time when they could have chosen to move away from the discomfort around loss.

There will be awkward moments in navigating grief. There will be days when it's easy to feel alone and misunderstood in the journey of loss. I invite you, even if it's challenging, to see the love between the lines.

Parenting through Grief

I never planned on being a single parent. If I hadn't met Michael, I would not have been one of those inspirational women who confidently choose to have a child on their own. I love being a mom, but I always believed I would have the framework of a loving partnership surrounding me as I made my way through the joys and challenges of parenting.

When Michael died, this too changed. Our long-term plan of me working part-time while Lucas was young, and Michael retiring in time to take over for the teen years, evaporated. My safety net of sanity, ready to catch me when I was at the end of my patience, disappeared. My sounding board and confidant turned into a vacuum of silence. The book-reading, bathtub-loving, bedtime magician was gone. My tag-team had left the game and I struggled to provide the love of two parents to a grieving child with my compromised self already low on energy.

I wasn't able to be two parents. I could only be one. I asked for help, which was thankfully available. My mom, just as she did when Michael was ill, graciously came from Alaska whenever I needed her, and the community of friends surrounding us made the first months doable. But more than anything, Lucas needed me. He had endured the disturbed routines and fractured chaos of Michael's last month, and more than anything in his grief, he needed his mom.

I showed up in the best way I knew how within my haze of grief, but I quickly learned it wasn't going to be perfect. Not that it ever was, but this was a whole new level of imperfection. Lucas probably watched too much television and it's no secret that he ate too many quesadillas. But the basics were covered.

He was heard.

We were connected.

We played.

We snuggled.

We cried.

And when my patience bank was empty, and I raised my voice or otherwise expressed my irritability, I tried to remember to reach out for help; to ask a neighbor to look after Lucas so I could take a walk and regain my composure.

Over time, I learned where the sticky spots were. I learned that everything Michael used to do and which had now fallen to me were the places where I lost my patience the most. It wasn't that I didn't want to read twenty books at bedtime; it was that I didn't think it was my job because that was when I used to make a cup of tea and write. I wasn't against sticking my feet in the tub and hanging out for bath time, but I didn't want to because I was so used to doing the dishes then. It never occurred to me to make the bedtime routine a connected, relaxing time for both of us.

There were other times as well: the inevitable emptiness at dinnertime and the homework that was suddenly a struggle when it never had been before. I learned to uncover the tough spots, and it was no surprise to discover they were the times in which we were both missing Michael. No wonder they were hard.

We found a new rhythm, and thankfully we also found support by attending Me, Too a six-week family grief group offered by hospice. Here, I learned the language of grief from a child's perspective. I learned that children grieve in different developmental stages and they grieve through the language of play. It was invaluable for me to know and learn. It was also critical for both of us to know we weren't alone, that others faced the same challenges.

I learned that mostly Lucas needed connection and routine. It wasn't until a full year later that I saw him express his grief more outwardly. It may have had to do with him moving into a more concrete cognitive stage and understanding that Michael wasn't coming back. I also wonder if he was subconsciously waiting for me to have it a little bit more together before he expressed his own need to grieve.

Either way, he began to grieve, and I have to admit that I was relieved. I was relieved, and then shortly after I was overwhelmed. I worried that I didn't know how to fully support him. His grief showed up as feelings of isolation from his peers, as loneliness when he wanted Michael, and as anger that came out of the blue. Of course, as with all great parenting lessons, I had to take time to look at my own feelings, especially anger, before I could support him in finding safe ways to let the big energy out.

Luckily, we again found support and a place to safely learn what it meant to be a child and an adult facing loss. We were blessed enough to have The Dougy Center for Grieving Children, a national training center for assisting families through grief, right here in Portland. This wonderful resource trains facilitators to provide grief support services for families all over the country. We attended for a year, with Lucas mostly engaging in big energy play and me mostly engaging in sharing tears or laughter in the parent support groups. We found a place where it was safe to grieve and where we weren't alone. After a year, Lucas told me he was ready to be a "regular kid" again and that he wanted to take a break. So we closed our participation, knowing we can return if we ever need a second run at it or if we hit a new developmental stage that needs a different kind of connection or process.

I learned so much from the group and from the other parents that now we seem to be in a pretty even phase of grieving. I don't feel as challenged by the aspects of parenting that relate to grief as much as I am simply trying to keep up with the normal parental dance of growing and changing with each new age and stage.

I'm a good mom, and I'm also human. I make mistakes. I know I can't be a single mom in a silo of aloneness. I need community. I reach out often. I maintain connections to others who are also parenting through grief. And most importantly, I attend to self-care because the times I stumble are the times when I'm tired, stretched, need to cry, or haven't slept or eaten well. I give myself a lot of empathy and forgive myself for when I forget we've been through a lot. I try my best to acknowledge Lucas's feelings rather than rushing in to fix whatever is wrong. I often find what he needs most is to know he's heard. I reflect back to him what I see, "You're feeling sad," "You feel like the only one at school who doesn't have a dad," "You wish your dad was here." The less I try to change what he's feeling, the stronger we both are in understanding the process of grief.

If you are parenting, I invite you first to be gentle with yourself, to bolster your days with self-care. I invite you to reach out for help from family and friends. I also found it invaluable to connect with others going through a similar experience. Both The Dougy Center and the National Alliance for Grieving Children are listed in the resources section of this book and can assist you in finding grief support in your area.

I invite you to embrace the imperfections and to find a place of empathy where you can stand both in your own shoes and those of your child while you ask what each of you are feeling and what you need right now. I invite you to stop, just for a moment, and remember you are a parent doing his or her best, and to remember who your child is: a young person learning how to express grief.

I invite you to identify the sticky spots. These spots might be hard simply because they're a new role. I invite you to experiment with these times—keep a little of the routine but mix it up with your own spice. Toss a game in where dinner conversation used to be. Put your feet in the tub. Let your child or children lead you to play when you can't find your way. Reflect what you see them feeling. They often know the way out of grief easier than we do, with our attachments to the past and future. I invite you to let them teach you to grieve in the moment.

Body, Mind, and Soul – The Art of Self-Care

The airline advice of putting your own oxygen mask on before helping others is indeed true, yet so hard to carry out when everyone else's needs seem so pressing. There's always lunch to be packed, laundry to be done, bills to be paid, dog food to be purchased, or the volunteer shift to be filled. If we're not careful, there will always be something else that needs to be done before self-care. Only after all that gets done, we feel, will there be time to relax and look after ourselves. But I learned slowly that putting self-care first rather than last made a huge difference as to whether I was able to get through another day with patience and a shred of grace.

Grief wore me down physically, emotionally, mentally. It took a long time for me to understand that taking care of myself demanded more priority than ever before. I needed to be outside every day. I needed to find a way to eat nourishing food at a time when cooking felt impossible. I needed to sit quietly and read something inspirational. I needed yoga. I needed time with friends who could lift me up and make me laugh. Most of all, I needed rest. I needed to put self-care on the list before anything else. I needed to remember that I was the glue holding this precarious ship together.

At times, staying intact required help. There were the obvious things I could do for myself, those things that had nurtured me in the past and still formed the foundation for self-care, but I also reached out. I found a healthcare provider who understood grief and assisted me in finding physical balance through resting my worn adrenals and supporting my nervous system. I found a grief support group and learned the essential nature of being with others walking a similar path. I found a spiritual community that touched my heart and lifted my spirits. And as much as I could, I let myself rest and recover.

I invite you to open to what nourishes you. I invite you to put self-care first on your list for the day. I invite you to reach out to find support from a healthcare provider, a massage therapist, a nutritionist, or a friend. I invite you to trust you will recover and your energy will come back. It can be as simple as stopping to breathe. Whatever you choose, I invite you to nourish yourself first.

Overwhelm, Future Tripping, and Taking One Step at a Time

The one action that has caused me to lose balance more than any other is the trap affectionately termed by my grief counselor as "future tripping." It's the dangerous path I go down when I'm triggered by something overwhelming, like big financial decisions, Lucas being sick or breaking a bone, or figuring out self-employment taxes. On this path, I question myself about what will happen if I make a wrong decision that starts a cascade of calamity, impossible to stop. It usually happens when I encounter something new and feel ill-prepared to answer all the questions I think are urgent and need to be answered in that exact moment. It comes in the times when I wish Michael were here to talk with me. It comes at times when I am alone with decisions that used to be shared.

As it turns out, most paths are not determined by one large decision made in the throes of anxiety. All the issues that overwhelmed me shortly after Michael died turned out to be solved by a step-by-step process of finding a solution. I've found that making lists and planning out a series of steps helps the process immensely. I also discovered that when I admit I don't know something, it's easier to find help than if I buy into the belief that I should figure it out on my own at the very same moment when I think the world might collapse.

The loss of a partner brings up overwhelming tasks that otherwise would never have been tackled alone. It wreaks havoc on events that might seem mundane like deciding on health insurance, filing taxes, or signing a rental contract for a new office. New decisions can bring up anxiety, and my anxiety trigger is a lot higher having experienced the trauma of death. I was always waiting for the drama to explode, the garage door to break, the computer to crash.

As one who still occasionally still falls for this trip, I invite you to trust you have everything you need to make wise decisions. Calamity is not as close as you think.

Space and Open Air

Getting outside always helped me feel better. Two days after Michael died, we piled into the car and drove to the beach. It seemed a little irreverent at the time. Perhaps we should have stayed home, shrouded in solemnity. But we needed the big sky, the sand, and the healing pull of the ocean waves. Nearly three years later, I can still attest to the power of nature to pull me out of grief and into a broader view. Whether it's the shift in perspective, the change in scenery, or the presence of fresh air, nature always heals.

I invite you today to step outside. See what touches your senses. I invite you to get outdoors and move your body. Let the rhythm of your breath pull you up a hill, round a bend, or in close to a stream. I invite you to stand at night by the edge of a lake, looking out at the stars, and to wake the next morning to dawn shimmering through the trees. It can be any size step outside— whether a tentative walk into a wooded place near your home or a grand-scale adventure to a red-rocked canyon framed by the stunning brightness of a blue sky. Any movement toward a world in a state of constant growth will remind you that you too can and will shift with the seasons.

Writing a New Script

For so many of the early days of grief, I felt like I was on the wrong movie set. The plot lines and characters had all changed and I was paralyzed under the lights, facing the camera with absolutely no idea what to do or say. It took me a while to realize a new script wasn't going to be delivered. The only one who was going to write new lines was me. Slowly, I learned to create a new script. Every day I tried to do something that made me feel alive and with purpose. For me those things were writing, singing, and long walks. For you it may be skydiving, accounting, and bubble baths. We get to choose, and we only have to do a little bit each day.

I invite you to think about some small thing that would bring you alive today. If nothing comes, as was the case for me in the beginning, do what made you feel alive before grief came in the door. I did yoga, took hikes in nature, organized drawers, and trusted the inspiration would come.

What is it that brings you alive, or sparks a shift in your energy? I invite you to lean in, just a little, and trust the movement will follow. Maybe even add a new soundtrack to accompany the new script you are writing. You can write your new script one word at a time, even one letter at a time. The storyline always has room for change.

Joy, Happiness, Guilt, and Betrayal

It's okay to be happy. In the midst of grief, it's a rare blessing to feel joy. Happiness and expressions of joy are not a betrayal to the memory of your loved one. That being said, it's completely normal to feel like joy, happiness, and bliss are foreign, maybe even dangerous, emotions. I remember thinking to myself, "What if I'm so happy that I forget him?" And, "What will people think if they see me laughing?" I was holding this place inside myself of believing that laughter betrayed the love I had for him. To be fully transparent, I'll share that I believed people might think I was completely fine if I expressed happiness, and therefore I was no longer in need of support.

Turns out those moments of laughter, smiling, and happiness were rays of sunshine in a life that for a long time was mostly clouds and rain. It didn't mean I didn't still need a raincoat; just that I could take full advantage of the current weather if it was sunny.

Occasionally I walk a razor's edge of not wanting to be happy because I don't want to admit that I can be happy without him. I don't want to make it acceptable that he died. Being happy, expressing joy, living the full experience of my life, means I have to let my life with him go. What I finally realized was I can bring his memory into the happiness with us. I can now enjoy a moment of loving something, especially with Lucas, and think to myself, "Michael would have loved this!" In this way his memory comes with us, but does not hold us back.

Sometimes when I'm joyful or excited, I experience a strange phenomenon of crashing into the awareness that Michael won't be there to celebrate with me when I get home. I miss him when I'm happy. Now I try to share my joy with others and ask them to celebrate with me. I'm discovering how to fill the spaces where he's missing.

Accepting a new life that I love, even without him, means I'm also accepting that he's dead. His death is real, and yet three years later it's still hard to believe. I continually have to tell myself it's okay to move toward life and laughter. Expressing joy often means tears will come with yet another layer of loss. He isn't here to see me shine as I embrace a new career. He isn't here to see Lucas in his first basketball game, or acting in a play. I know he would be thrilled for us and I can accept that he would want us to be happy and live. If I had died first, I would have wanted him to live fully. I would have wanted him, above all else, to teach our son joy. So when I'm stuck and holding back from happiness, I put myself in his shoes. What would he say? Would he deny us happiness? And his memory appears, smiling out at me through the folds of my consciousness, telling me to live, love, and embrace joy.

I invite you to notice the moments when you feel happy, even if they are fleeting and far between. Notice these moments and feel them. See if the awareness draws more happiness to you.

You are the only one who can give yourself permission to feel joy.

Stepping Forward in Faith

My faith was shaken many times during Michael's illness, death, and the grief that followed. I wondered how an experience so terrible could happen to our family. In my anger, I at times stumbled in my faith. It was hard to believe in a loving force in the universe when the one thing I loved the most was taken away from me. I was lost and my faith felt tenuous.

I knew I had a choice to perceive the circumstances of my life either as a personal affront from God or as an unfortunate tragedy held within a larger container of love. I was able to choose love when I remembered the overwhelming presence of peace that surrounded us when Michael died. There was love supporting us, both in a spiritual sense and from those who held us close. This love that surrounded death became a touchstone for my own impetus to continue moving forward in faith.

I know that tragic events happen in our lives. I know that my perception of God or a loving presence that surrounds us has to include the reality that terrible things happen to wonderful people every day. Every moment. Every second.

And I know that I have a choice in where to put my faith. I have a choice as to whether to let love infuse my life or to turn away from love.

In writing about faith, I can only describe my own experience. Faith is a very personal journey for each of us. Whether we draw faith from a spiritual path, a religious tradition, or a connection to our common humanity, I believe the supportive force that emanates from all of these is love. We can see love in everything and this love can be as present in the challenging times as in the celebrations.

I invite you, whatever the roots of your faith, or even in absence of faith, to look for love. You might see it in the unexpected kindness of a stranger, or hear it in a song that touches your heart. The taste of it may come alive in a meal shared with friends, or in the fresh scent of a gently tended flower. You may receive its touch from a comforting embrace, or it may be present in your own hand as you reach out to another. I believe it's always there, somewhere, waiting for us to notice and move toward it. If grief is the loss of a place where we put our love, then healing comes from filling that space once again.

I invite you to choose to see love.

Afterword

The journal pages of this manuscript sat dormant in my computer for a year and a half. I put it aside, labeling it as worthwhile only for my own healing. I never imagined I would take the steps to have it published. It is similar to how it didn't seem possible to take so many of the other steps I have taken over the past three years since Michael's death. But steps forward are what make a life, and this book is no different.

A graceful synchronicity led me to the right editor, who showed me that my work wasn't just for me, but for anyone who needed an inside view of grief. The writing was healing for me, but the reading may be healing for others.

Whoever you are, if you've read this far, I hope this book has been supportive of you.

Perhaps you are grieving the loss of your spouse or some other loved one and needed to read a similar journey to reassure you that you aren't crazy. This is for you, and I'm here to say you are normal. Your expression of grief is normal. You are not crazy. You are living through the impossibility of loss. Grief is an expected response to death, but you will also need support, especially in those times when you feel weary, stuck, or alone. It's normal to grieve, and it's okay to seek help.

Or maybe you are close to someone who has lost a loved one and you have read this as a gift to them, to be exposed to the things they can't even begin to tell you are a part of their daily life for fear that you may not understand. Thank you for supporting them on their journey.

Or maybe you are one of those brave souls who are already a part of the conversation about grief, loss, illness, death, and dying; a conversation so hidden in our culture. I am grateful for you and know you will support many who need compassion for their cause.

I wrote this book because it was the book I needed to read and couldn't find. I knew there must be other people looking for this same book. The writing was healing, but it also speaks to the commonalities of grief lived by so many but that remain unspoken outside of therapy rooms or grief groups. It is a story not only of the grief that comes through death, but the grief that comes through many of the losses we experience by being human.

It's been nearly two years since I wrote the last journal entry of a year of grief. Much of this time has been similar to that first year, but with a slight brightening of each day. I can't say that I'm "over" grieving Michael. I will always miss him. There will be days where I continue to grieve and mourn. But I am now fully engaged in a life without his physical presence. I am healing, and I am learning to fill my heart with all the things in this world here to love. I am looking forward now, leaning into all of the experiences still left to unfold.

It's funny. In retrospect, I don't think I ever imagined there would be a happy ending to this story. It's not the classic "happily ever after" ending, but more the "happy and steadily moving forward no matter what life tosses in the mix" kind of ending.

In truth, we are all well.

Lucas is thriving. He sings and hums spontaneously, which for me is an undeniable mark of a happy person. He is an easygoing nine-year-old who loves sports, acting, math, and tickle fights. He grieves still, especially in the times when Michael was most present in his life—bedtime, bath time, roughhousing, bike rides, movies, and Legos. He says what he misses most is the way his dad laughed and how he made him feel safe. He has been changed by this loss, I know, and I also know it has strengthened him in ways that have yet to be revealed. He is wise beyond his years and filled with compassion.

Leit has found his rhythm too, and is a bright spot on our calendar when we schedule a family dinner or adventure day. He didn't have to choose to stay close here in Portland, but I'm grateful he's here, showing up as a big brother, adventure-maker, and chef extraordinaire. The days we spent together caring for Michael created the bedrock of our connection that carries us beyond the ties of our blended family. Now we are family; no other explanation needed.

Alta gets to be a dog again. She spent the first years of her life absorbing and comforting illness and grief. We adopted her just two weeks before Michael was diagnosed, and I can't help but think she's the most therapeutic dog that ever lived. I had a friend remark to me not long ago that it's time to tell Alta she can just be a dog now. She can spend as much time chasing squirrels and barking at skateboards as she does comforting her humans. She doesn't have to carry so much of the burden. I tell her that every once in a while, but more importantly, I ease her burden by needing her less.

And indeed, I need less as I live more. My life feels full, engaged, and on purpose. I'm still writing, but I've also started my own practice, focusing mainly on parent coaching and grief coaching. This was the dream I was on my way to fulfilling that fall when Michael was diagnosed. I am grateful every day for my work of being a companion to others in the process of searching for insight or navigating transitions on this journey of life.

I haven't yet sold the house, mostly in an effort to keep the steady support of Lucas's elementary school and the connection to community. We house-hunt a lot though, still trusting that just the right one is out there for us to create our next home. In addition to looking for houses, I'm looking for other matches in life, open to the possibility of new love. I've dated a little, learned a lot, shed some tears, and laughed along the way.

I've found my tribe—friends, fellow widows, a talented grief counselor, and caring neighbors. I still have times where I ache with loss, and yet have learned to trust that the ache subsides and joy rushes in to replace it every time. As my friend Jamie, co-founder of our very small but thriving Fun Young Widows club, says, "The most important things to know about grief are that it gets better and to never try to do it alone." It does get better, and I can't imagine having walked this road alone. I am grateful for all the support from friends, family, and community that engage Lucas and I in living fully authentic and connected lives.

I'll end with a reflection on how our life has unfolded by sharing a poignant moment that happened on a Thanksgiving trip to Costa Rica this year. The foresight to know that we needed to leave town and shake up the holiday scenery was a big acknowledgement of our healing. We cashed in the rest of our frequent flyer miles and met the challenge of international travel. It was a huge leap of faith for me to trust I had the capacity to meet a larger world, after having finally settled into some solid ground at home.

But the bigger step was when Lucas convinced me to go ziplining in the jungle. I'm afraid of heights, so the thought terrified me, but I knew it was a way to step courageously into something new after so much time spent in the hesitancy of anxiety and grief. When we got to the top of the mountain, with ten miles of zip lines and platforms stretching out before us, Lucas was first in line. He didn't hesitate, jumping into the trees with a holler and a smile. I knew I had no choice but to follow him. I stood there on the wooden platform, clinging to my safety line and shaking visibly from head to toe. I didn't want to leave the solidity of the mountain. I was scared, overwhelmed, anxious, and unsure. But my son was ahead of me, flying through the jungle, and I had no choice but to leave the ground behind and step into the air below.

Turns out I flew.

Resources

General Books and Resources on Grief

Alan D. Wolfelt, PhD. *Understanding Your Grief: Ten Essential Touchstones.* Fort Collins, Colorado: Companion Press, 2003.

Christina Rasmussen. *Second firsts: Live, Laugh, and Love Again.* Carlsbad, California: Hay House Inc., 2013. www.secondfirsts.com

C.S. Lewis. *A Grief Observed.* New York: Harper One, 2001.

Kate Braestrup. *Here If You Need Me: A True Story.* New York: Back Bay Books, 2007

Becky Aikman. *Saturday Night Widows: The Adventures of Six Friends Remaking Their Lives.* New York: Random House, 2013

Grief Coaching: Carrie Doubts, MA, PCC, www. lifesnextchaptercoaching.com

Modern Widows Club: www.modernwidowsclub.com

Resources for Grieving Children

The Dougy Center. The National Center for Grieving Children and Families. www.dougy.org

National Alliance for Grieving Children. www.nation-alallianceforgrievingchildren.org

Me, Too – Supporting Children and Families in Grief www.oregonhospice.org/me-too

Earl A. Grollman. *Talking about Death: A Dialogue Between Parent and Child.* Boston: Beacon Press, 1990.

Leo Buscaglia, PhD. *The Fall of Freddie the Leaf: A Story of Life for All Ages.* Thorofare, New Jersey: Slack Incorporated, 1982.

Pat Thomas. *I Miss You: A First Look at Death.* Hauppauge, New York: Barron's Educational Series, Inc., 2001.

Permissions

Acknowledgements

Thank you to my mom, sister, and Leit. Your care, guidance, love, and laughter were ever present as we made our way through the hardest of days. And for Lucas whose bright spirit pulls me forward into a future full of adventure. I am in awe of the grace, joy, and endurance of our family.

A big thank you to Michelle, Carrie, Matthew, Susan, Janet, Melanie, Deb, Nani, and Angela for reading this work early on in its roughest form and encouraging me to find a way to put it out into the world. Your support, feedback, and reflections were essential to the process.

Karen Lacey - you knew this book was yours to help publish after the first read. I'm grateful you saw the message I needed to share and helped make it readable and beautiful. Thank you for the skilled editing, unending support, keen eye for cliché's, and book midwifery talents. And to Alex Hughes and Ann Decker for your attention to detail and reserves of patience during copy-editing and design.

And to the wise circle of women who laughed, cried, listened, danced, and walked with me over the last three years. You are irreplaceable in my heart. Thank you.

About the Author

Carole Marie Downing, ND, MA is a writer, coach and facilitator committed to inspiring and facilitating conversations about embracing life after loss.

Carole holds a Nursing Doctorate from the University of Colorado. As a nurse she provided care in the areas of pain management, hospice care, integrative medicine and nursing education. She also received a Master's degree in Spiritual Psychology with a post-graduate certificate in Consciousness, Health and Healing from the University of Santa Monica.

She currently works as a coach, supporting individuals through the journey of grief and specializes in working with parents who have experienced the death of a partner or spouse. In addition to her coaching practice, she is available for speaking engagements and also provides workshops on writing as a tool for healing and viewing grief through the lens of gratitude.

She lives in Portland, Oregon with her son and their dog Alta.

Find out more about her work and coaching practice online at cmdowning.com

CPSIA information can be obtained
at www.ICGtesting.com
Printed in the USA
FSHW011253221220
77086FS